The American Novel series provides students of American literature with introductory critical guides to the great works of American literature. Each volume begins with a substantial introduction by a distinguished authority on the text, giving details of the work's composition, publication history, and contemporary reception, as well as a survey of the major critical trends and readings from first publication to the present. This overview is followed by a group of new essays, each specially commissioned from a leading scholar in the field, which together constitute a forum of interpretative methods and prominent contemporary ideas on the text. There are also helpful guides to further reading. Specifically designed for undergraduates, the series will be a powerful resource for anyone engaged in the critical analysis of major American novels and other important texts.

Feminist literary criticism has fundamentally revised our understanding of Sarah Orne Jewett and *The Country of the Pointed Firs*. What Jewett's place in American literature will be at the end of the twentieth century remains to be seen, however, and the essays in this volume offer a radically new view of her significance. Building on feminist analyses of Jewett's role in the female literary culture of her day, the distinctive formal qualities of her fiction, and the importance of her subject matter, the essays also historicize Jewett's work in the frames of reference that have emerged as important in recent critical study. Most strikingly, they reveal how deeply racialized and nationalist are the categories through which Jewett – as a participant in the culture industry and a highly successful writer negotiating gendered institutions – constructs her local solidarities. The currently received ways of understanding Jewett – as a regionalist and as a woman writer – are unified in an account of her involvement in the process through which a national culture was constructed at the turn of the century. Less celebratory than feminist criticism of Jewett has been so far, the essays in this volume are nevertheless deeply respectful of her craft and seriousness. As a group they present the most historically informed and critically appreciative readings of *The Country of the Pointed Firs* published to date.

NEW ESSAYS ON
THE COUNTRY OF THE POINTED FIRS

★ The American Novel ★

GENERAL EDITOR
Emory Elliott
University of California, Riverside

New Essays on The Country of the Pointed Firs

Edited by
June Howard
University of Michigan, Ann Arbor

CAMBRIDGE
UNIVERSITY PRESS

Published by the Press Syndicate of the University of Cambridge
The Pitt Building, Trumpington Street, Cambridge CB2 1RP
40 West 20th Street, New York, NY 10011-4211, USA
10 Stamford Road, Oakleigh, Melbourne 3166, Australia

© Cambridge University Press 1994

First published 1994

Printed in the United States of America

Library of Congress Cataloging-in-Publication Data
New essays on The country of the pointed firs / edited by June Howard.
p.   cm. – (The American novel)
Includes bibliographical references.
ISBN 0-521-41574-8 (hc). – ISBN 0-521-42602-2 (pb)
1. Jewett, Sarah Orne, 1849–1909. Country of the pointed firs.
2. Women and literature – United States – History – 19th century.
3. Maine – In literature.   I. Howard, June.   II. Series.
PS2132.C643N48   1994
813'.4 – dc20   93-33810
                                                              CIP

A catalog record for this book is available from the British Library.

ISBN 0-521-41574-8 hardback
ISBN 0-521-42602-2 paperback

Contents

v

Contents

Series Editor's Preface

In literary criticism the last twenty-five years have been particularly fruitful. Since the rise of the New Criticism in the 1950s,
which focused attention of critics and readers upon the text itself –
apart from history, biography, and society – there has emerged a
wide variety of critical methods which have brought to literary
works a rich diversity of perspectives: social, historical, political,
psychological, economic, ideological, and philosophical. While attention to the text itself, as taught by the New Critics, remains at
the core of contemporary interpretation, the widely shared assumption that works of art generate many different kinds of interpretation has opened up possibilities for new readings and new
meanings.

Before this critical revolution, many American novels had come
to be taken for granted by earlier generations of readers as having
an established set of recognized interpretations. There was a sense
among many students that the canon was established and that the
larger thematic and interpretative issues had been decided. The
task of the new reader was to examine the ways in which elements
such as structure, style, and imagery contributed to each novel's
acknowledged purpose. But recent criticism has brought these old
assumptions into question and has thereby generated a wide variety of original, and often quite surprising, interpretations of the
classics, as well as of rediscovered novels such as Kate Chopin's *The
Awakening*, which has only recently entered the canon of works
that scholars and critics study and that teachers assign their students.

The aim of *The American Novel* series is to provide students of
American literature and culture with introductory critical guides to

American novels now widely read and studied. Each volume is devoted to a single novel and begins with an introduction by the volume editor, a distinguished authority on the text. The introduction presents details of the novel's composition, publication history, and contemporary reception, as well as a survey of the major critical trends and readings from first publication to the present. This overview is followed by four or five original essays, specifically commissioned from senior scholars of established reputation and from outstanding younger critics. Each essay presents a distinct point of view, and together they constitute a forum of interpretative methods and of the best contemporary ideas on each text.

It is our hope that these volumes will convey the vitality of current critical work in American literature, generate new insights and excitement for students of the American novel, and inspire new respect for and new perspectives upon these major literary texts.

Emory Elliott
University of California, Riverside

Introduction:
Sarah Orne Jewett
and the Traffic in Words

JUNE HOWARD

S ARAH Orne Jewett published her first short story when she was eighteen years old, in 1868. The acceptance of "Jenny Garrow's Lovers" by a Boston weekly periodical was quickly followed by others; by the time Jewett turned twenty-one, she had published three more stories and two poems – including a story in the *Atlantic Monthly,* the leading literary periodical of the day (which paid her the respectable sum of fifty dollars). Although her strongest work was done later, in the 1880s and '90s, from that first pseudonymous publication until her disabling carriage accident in 1902 not a year passed without something Jewett had written appearing in print. In thirty-five years Jewett published more than two hundred magazine and newspaper pieces, ten collections of short stories and sketches, four books for children, and five novels. And despite the occasional negative notice, her work was consistently praised by critics during her lifetime; it has been admired by at least some readers and scholars ever since. Yet estimates of her importance in American literary history have varied. A certain language of diminution – her work is characterized as "small," "exquisite," "minor" – appears from the first in the commentary on Jewett and becomes the keynote of professional literary critics' assessments of her work as the twentieth century passes. Our understanding of Jewett's work has been profoundly revised in recent years, however, and we may again be ready to take seriously Willa Cather's often-quoted assertion: "If I were asked to name three American books which have the possibility of a long, long life, I would say at once, 'The Scarlet Letter,' 'Huckleberry Finn,' and 'The Country of the Pointed Firs.'"[1]

One point that has never been disputed, however, is that *The*

Country of the Pointed Firs is Jewett's finest book – even, perhaps, a kind of summation of what is best in her work. Her reputation had been firmly established for many years when it appeared in 1896, first as a serial in the *Atlantic Monthly* and then in book form. It was a certainty that the book would be respectfully reviewed. But the response went far beyond that; most critics recognized immediately that Jewett's seventeenth book exceeded her ordinarily high standard. It was praised for intensifying the qualities consistently found in Jewett's work: for its vivid portrait of the human and natural landscape of rural New England, for the beauty of its style, for its capacity to evoke a sense of deep significance in everyday life. These are topics that, in various formulations, continue to concern critics today. Alice Brown, herself a regional writer of distinction, wrote a review that began, *"The Country of the Pointed Firs* is the flower of a sweet, sane knowledge of life, and an art so elusive that it smiles up at you while you pull aside the petals, vainly probing its heart" and went on to say that "the pointed firs have their roots in the ground of national being; they are index fingers to the stars. A new region unrolls before you like a living map." After praising specific characters a ' ᵊnisodes, many of them the same as those receiving attentioɪ ɪn the pages of this volume, Brown concludes, "No such beautiful and perfect work has been done for many years; perhaps no such beautiful work has ever been done in America."[2]

In contrast, the anonymous reviewer in the *Bookman* comments favorably on the "picturesque delineation of character, the writer's close contact with nature, and her appreciative insight, [which] all contribute a reality and charm to the book which are very convincing," but concludes that "the little volume comes to its quiet ending, leaving the impression that, suggestive and delightful as such books are, they cannot, save in rare instances, leave any deep impression. Miss Jewett possesses the artistic power, the knowledge, and the self-control to venture more. These delicate sketches of life hold the same place in literature as do their counterparts in painting, but no artist can rest an enduring popularity on such trifles light as air."[3] No other reviewer sounds so dissatisfied, but many characterize the book, and Jewett's work in general, in ways that suggest they view it as somehow inconsequential. One writes that this "little book is marked by good taste" and is "at times gently pathetic, at others delicately humorous" and "always free from exaggeration." Others refer to Jewett's "slender song" and slight material.[4] This note is struck even by Jewett's literary friends and acquaintances. For example, in a reminiscence written some years later, Henry James expresses intense, yet distinctly limited and even condescending admiration for her work: Jewett is "mistress of an art of fiction all her own, even though of a minor compass," with a "beautiful little quantum of achievement" that might have lived up to her gift if not for the "premature and overdarkened close of her young course of production."[5] Jewett's career was, certainly, deplorably shortened by her death at the age of fifty-nine; but even in comparison with James's own remarkably long life as a writer, it is difficult to think of her career as unfulfilled. There is, we will see, something important to be understood in the curiously mingled tone of respect and depreciation found in so many assessments of Sarah Orne Jewett.

Suggestions that Jewett's work is fine but slight are usually linked to her regional subject matter and often (at least by implication) to her status as a woman writing mostly about women. The sources and significance of such suggestions can be understood only against the broad canvas of American literary history. In what follows I situate Jewett's career, and the trajectory of her reputation, in the history of American literary culture since the mid-nineteenth century. Jewett emerged as a writer through a small but very influential New England literary elite that had been consolidated during the 1850s, by an earlier generation. She worked successfully within this tradition even as it was being transformed into a broader middle-class American culture. But changes already at work during her lifetime reshaped literary institutions in ways that rendered Jewett's distinctive version of the genteel tradition less and less readable; attitudes that developed in the professionalized study of language and literature in universities, in particular, meant that Jewett's place in the revised American literary canon created in the 1920s was much reduced. Since the 1960s, another shift in attitudes has reversed the downward trend in Jewett's reputation. The canon has been challenged for its exclusions, analyzed from the perspectives of race, class, gender, and sexuality,

3

and has been opened up to new authors and concerns. And as has happened across the humanities, and increasingly in the social sciences, new approaches to the understanding of language, culture, and society – what is often called "theory" – have led to revised notions of the scholar's tasks. It remains to be seen whether these are signs that yet another disciplinary order is emerging.

Feminist literary criticism, an important part of this most recent and still contested transformation, has fundamentally revised our understanding of Jewett, but what her place in American literature will be at the end of the twentieth century remains to be seen. Feminist critics have recovered information about Jewett's role in the female literary culture of her day, articulated the distinctive formal qualities of her fiction, and insisted upon the importance of her subject matter. This introduction and the other essays in this volume build most immediately and crucially on that body of work, but they also represent a new departure. Deliberately revisiting the familiar landscapes of Jewett criticism, we historicize in frames of reference that have emerged as important since 1985 and offer a radically revised view of Jewett's significance. Most strikingly, this volume reveals how deeply racialized and nationalist are the categories through which Jewett constructs her local solidarities. It also shows her as a participant in the culture industry, a highly successful writer negotiating a nexus of gendered institutions for producing literary meanings and commodities. Thus the currently received ways of understanding Jewett – as a regionalist and as a woman writer – are unified in an account of her implication in the process through which, at the turn into the twentieth century, a national culture was constituted. Less celebratory than feminist criticism of Jewett has been so far, it is nevertheless deeply respectful of her craft and seriousness; the essays in this volume seem to me to constitute the most historically informed and critically appreciative readings of *The Country of the Pointed Firs* published to date.

Theodora Sarah Orne Jewett was born in 1849, in South Berwick, Maine, a town of about five thousand inhabitants some ten miles from the Atlantic Ocean along the Piscataqua River. At the time of her birth, four generations of Jewetts lived in her paternal grandfather's distinguished house on the village square (built in 1774 and purchased from its original owner in 1819). Not long afterward, her father, Theodore Herman Jewett, built a separate, smaller residence next door, and Sarah and her sisters, Mary and Caroline, grew up there. Her grandfather was a retired shipowner and a prosperous merchant, her father a doctor, her uncle a merchant and later a banker; her close-knit extended family included most of the town's leadership, and its connections reached into other New England communities.[6] Jewett was deeply attached to her home in South Berwick, and biographers have, plausibly, identified it as an emblem of her family's solid social and financial standing and of her rootedness in family and community. After the deaths of her grandfather, father, and uncle, Jewett returned to live in the "great house" and made it her primary residence from the mid-1880s until the end of her life.[7]

Jewett's health during her childhood was poor, and she attended school irregularly, although she did graduate from the Berwick Academy in 1866. From Jewett's autobiographical writing, we know that the many days she spent out of the classroom, driving through the countryside with her father as he made rounds for his rural medical practice, were formative for her; they served as an important source of her intimate knowledge of and sympathy for the human and natural landscapes of Maine. She credited her father with educating her as an observer, as well as guiding her wide reading and advising her about her writing, until his sudden death in 1878. She dedicated *Country By-Ways* (1881) to him: "My dear father; my dear friend; the best and wisest man I ever knew; who taught me many lessons and showed me many things as we went together along the country by-ways."[8] Jewett's expressions of affection for her mother, Caroline Perry Jewett, are more conventional, and what has been written about the relationship between the two is more speculative; we know, however, that her mother and grandmother introduced her early to female authors such as Austen and Eliot who were immediately congenial.[9] She was close to her sisters, and they corresponded voluminously when apart; she dedicated a book to each of them. Affectionate references to other family members fill her letters.

As Jewett grew up, others joined her family at the center of her emotional life. The historical record includes detailed information about the ever-widening circle of Jewett's friendships – with, to name only a few representative figures, Edith Haven Doe, a married woman living a mile away who spent time with all of the Jewett girls; Kate Birckhead of Newport, Rhode Island, one of several early "crushes" and the model for Kate Lancaster in *Deephaven;* Lily Munger, daughter of a Maine clergyman, younger than Jewett and recipient of a number of rather didactic letters during the late 1870s; and, most important, Annie Fields, who was her close companion from the early 1880s on. Even before she began spending a considerable portion of her time at Fields's homes in Boston and Manchester and journeying to Europe with her every few years, Jewett was scarcely secluded in South Berwick but traveled widely, visiting family and friends. She went frequently to Boston and Newport, stayed for some months during 1868 and 1869 with her mother's brother and his wife in Cincinnati, visited other sites in the Midwest, and saw the 1876 Centennial Exposition in Philadelphia while visiting her mother's relatives there. Jewett enjoyed both her particular friends and sociability in general; on one busy day during an 1878 visit to Washington, D.C., where a friend's husband was sitting in Congress, Jewett reported that she "assisted in receiving ninety callers in the afternoon, then attended a reception given by President Lincoln's son where she saw 'ever so many people we knew,' entertained dinner guests, and went to a White House reception in the evening."[10] As a young woman Jewett formed connections that would continue to the end of her life, and she constantly added to their number.

Neither the institution of visiting – Jewett spent two months with her friend in Washington – nor such intense, durable bonds of female friendship are familiar to us in the late twentieth century. But historians enable us to make the leap of understanding necessary to see how fundamental they were in the fabric of Jewett's life. Carroll Smith-Rosenberg broke the ground for the study of nineteenth-century female friendship in a 1975 essay titled "The Female World of Love and Ritual." Depicting a social world characterized by sharply differentiated gender roles in the family and in society as a whole, producing an "emotional segregation of women and men," she finds a correspondingly strong, "unselfconscious pattern of single-sex or homosocial networks." The diaries and letters Smith-Rosenberg examines show relatives and friends supporting one another in domestic work and in the rituals with which they surrounded marriage, childbirth, illness, and death, creating a female world of "mutual dependency and deep affection." Women wrote of "the joy and contentment they felt in one another's company, their sense of isolation and despair when apart. The regularity of their correspondence underlines the sincerity of such words." Smith-Rosenberg describes relationships ranging "from the supportive love of sisters, through the enthusiasms of adolescent girls, to sensual avowals of love by mature women," sometimes between women of similar ages and sometimes across generations. She notes that these intimate, long-lasting friendships "did not form isolated dyads but were normally part of highly integrated networks. Knowing one another, perhaps related to one another, they played a central role in holding communities and kin systems together."[11]

Subsequent historical research has suggested that Smith-Rosenberg overestimated the degree of gender segregation among middle-class Americans in the nineteenth century; certainly Jewett, whose life in any case extended well beyond the period Smith-Rosenberg examines, included men in her friendship networks.[12] But Jewett's biography confirms the existence and importance of these powerful bonds among women. Willa Cather wrote that "her friendships occupied perhaps the first place in her life."[13] Such connections both shaped daily life and carried deep spiritual significance. Jewett's sense of communion with friends and her religious faith were linked in her mind; in an often-quoted letter, with explicit allusion to the New Testament, she wrote, "There is something transfiguring in the best of friendship."[14] She believed that powerful bonds might even enable communication between the living and the dead; as Elizabeth Ammons has detailed in an essay titled "Jewett's Witches," Jewett, like others of her period, took spiritualism, and the possibility that a supernatural order left its traces within the natural, quite seriously.[15] The wide-ranging significance of these female bonds is a necessary context for understanding both the texture of Jewett's life and the centrality of relations among women in her fiction, including *The Country of the*

Pointed Firs. Reciprocally, her fiction provides a rich resource for recapturing the depth of meaning with which themes of hospitality and friendship can be imbued.

Women were at the center of Jewett's emotional life; whether we therefore think of her as a lesbian writer depends on how we define that category. In some sense the characterization is anachronistic. It was toward the end of the nineteenth century that the concept of lesbianism, in medical literature and individual consciousness, emerged in the United States and Great Britain; Jewett, her attitudes already formed, never defined her loving female friendships in that way. Sharon O'Brien has shown what a profound difference the single generation that divides Jewett from her protégé Willa Cather (born in 1873) makes. As O'Brien points out, in Jewett's 1897 story "Martha's Lady," for example, she "felt no need to cast one character as male when she presented a friendship marked by sensuality as well as spiritual and emotional intensity."[16] When Cather made a different choice and used a male narrator in a love story, Jewett thought of it simply as a mistake in craft rather than in terms of social acceptability. She wrote in a 1908 letter: "The lover is as well done as he could be when a woman writes in the man's character, – it must always, I believe, be something of a masquerade. I think it is safer to write about him as you did about the others, and not try to be he! And you could almost have done it as yourself – a woman could love her in the same protecting way."[17] Only three years later, when Annie Fields edited Jewett's letters, she was persuaded that it would be safer to delete affectionate nicknames and omit some letters – for fear people would "'read them wrong.'"[18] Clearly, Jewett's relation to modern sexual identities is oblique; just as clearly, she has a place among writers who portray intimacies and devotions that do not follow heterosexual scripts.

As Jewett became established as an author, her friendships increasingly drew her into the literary world. Those connections followed the initial success of her work; Jewett submitted her earliest stories and poems through the mail, to strangers. But she quickly enlisted editors as professional advisers and friends, offering them in her letters unstinted admiration and deference. In the early years of Jewett's career, the most important of these mentors was Horace Scudder, whom Richard Brodhead characterizes as "one of those nineteenth-century literary figures who seem to have belonged simultaneously to the management of every literary and cultural institution, and who integrated their workings in practical terms; as Houghton Mifflin's chief editor, he was also a manager of children's magazines, an eventual editor of the *Atlantic*, and a longtime member of the Massachusetts Board of Education."[19] Jewett was also close to William Dean Howells, who was for decades a central figure in the literary life of his time. While associate editor of the *Atlantic Monthly*, he rejected Jewett's first two submissions and accepted the third; he went on to serve as editor from 1871 to 1881 and later broadened his influence from a base in New York with the extensive Harper's publishing enterprise. Howells took the lead, supported by Scudder, in encouraging Jewett to produce her first novel, *Deephaven*, published in 1877. It is likely that it was Howells who introduced her to James and Annie Fields.

The significance of that introduction may not be apparent to all readers, for the Fieldses have been among the casualties of the twentieth-century revisions of the canon; but they were key figures in the genteel literary culture Jewett was joining. There was no publisher in nineteenth-century America more respected than James T. Fields. He built Ticknor and Fields into a strong house during the 1840s and '50s; Henry James wrote (long afterward, in the same reminiscence quoted earlier) that Fields "had a conception of possibilities of relation with his authors and contributors that I judge no other member of his body in all the land to have had. . . . Few were our native authors, and the friendly Boston house had gathered them in almost all."[20] Richard Brodhead describes Fields's contribution in equally striking, if less reverent, terms, writing that he "in effect pioneered the art of book promotion. He began the practice of advertising beyond local markets, thereafter making advertising into a central part of book production. . . . He converted reviewing into a form of advertising too, using his friendly relations with editors he advertised with to get them to give favorable notice to books he published."[21] The constitution of an American literary public depended both on the consolidation of cultural authority and on the creation of a market.

Fields's innovative ingenuity was thus devoted to the task of promoting fine American literature, a category whose existence could not be taken for granted in the mid-nineteenth century. It was a period in which, as Brodhead puts it, "the paying audience for imaginative writing was expanding."

> Fields found a way to identify a certain portion of that writing as distinguished – as of elevated quality, as of premium cultural value; then to build a market for that writing on the basis of that distinction. Fields solidified this differentiated category of the literary not only by printing the contemporary works that *were* the most distinguished, or that *were* the most highly literary (though his eye for such works is impressive); he established it too by devising ways to identify and confirm the literary as a difference before the market. His inventions in this regard include the production features he found to stamp on his books, features that both mark them off as separate from other books and confer on them an air of distinction – features like the Ticknor and Fields format of conspicuously good paper and handsome brown boards, promising that what is inside is serious and well-made.

Fields was also the second editor of the *Atlantic Monthly,* succeeding James Russell Lowell in 1861, not long after his publishing house had purchased the journal, and remaining as owner after he passed the editorship on to Howells in 1871. The journal, too, worked to confirm the authority of this elite literary establishment.

The literary salon over which Annie Fields presided in their home was an important part of the system. It continued even after her husband's retirement in 1871 and after his death in 1881. Willa Cather was introduced to Mrs. Fields and Miss Jewett in 1908; this is how she evokes the atmosphere of this unofficial institution:

> For a period of sixty years Mrs. Fields' Boston house, at 148 Charles Street, extended its hospitality to the aristocracy of letters and art. During that long stretch of time there was scarcely an American of distinction in art or public life who was not a guest in that house; scarcely a visiting foreigner of renown who did not pay his tribute there.
>
> It was not only men of letters, Dickens, Thackeray, and Matthew Arnold, who met Mrs. Fields' friends there; Salvini and Modjeska and Edwin Booth and Christine Nilsson and Joseph Jefferson and Ole Bull, Winslow Homer and Sargent, came and went, against

10

the background of closely united friends who were a part of the very Charles Street scene. Longfellow, Emerson, Whittier, Hawthorne, Lowell, Sumner, Norton, Oliver Wendell Holmes – the list sounds like something in a school-book; but in Mrs. Fields' house one came to believe that they had been very living people – to feel that they had not been long absent from the rooms so full of their thoughts, of their letters, their talk, their remembrances sent at Christmas to the hostess, or brought to her from foreign lands.[22]

The intensely retrospective tone of this memoir derives not just from the fact that Cather was writing in 1936 but also from her knowledge that she entered this world as it was closing. In 1908, Fields was seventy-four, and Jewett, at fifty-eight, was only a year from her death. (Fields lived until 1915.) Cather is looking back toward the making of the American literary classics of her own schooling, fully aware that the power of this genteel culture is gone and that even as she writes the canon is being remade.

The educational system played a central role in the constitution of a small body of New England writing as a national literature, and that role was itself the invention of the cultural "aristocracy" Cather describes. Jewett's mentor Horace Scudder was one of those who actively promoted the adoption of American classics in the schools. During the 1860s and '70s, Ticknor and Fields underwent a series of transformations through changes in the partnership – they can be traced, in fact, through the sometimes complicated publishing information to be found in first editions of Jewett's early books – and by the 1880s Houghton Mifflin had bought the firm's list and was carrying forward, less exclusively but still distinctively, the project of publishing fine American literature.[23] Scudder issued inexpensive editions of New England authors for use in the schools, simultaneously securing an enormous market for textbooks and acting on his "deeply Arnoldian belief in the spiritual value of literary classics and their supreme social significance in a democracy."[24] To many elite New Englanders, and other Americans as well, it seemed that the foundations of social order were under threat from big business and class conflict, ignorant plutocrats and uncivilized immigrants. Scudder believed that by reading these works an increasingly heterogeneous and disorderly populace would be elevated and Americanized. This faith in

11

culture in the normative sense, in Arnold's "study and pursuit of perfection" through uplifting aesthetic experiences, as a way of harmonizing the body politic and preserving social and moral order, was a powerful force among middle- and upper-class Americans of the late nineteenth century.[25]

Recent cultural histories may make literary scholars more self-conscious about the distinctions we habitually draw among cultural practices, and in particular about the link between what Lawrence Levine calls the "sacralization of culture" and authority in a class-stratified society.[26] Brodhead connects the New England literary Victorians with that process when he writes, "Fields the canon-former and institution-builder is the agent, in the literary domain, of a general social process – its results are everywhere in the late nineteenth century, but he reminds us that it began in mid-century – through which American culture was reorganized on a more steeply hierarchical plan, featuring sharp gradations of levels of cultural value."[27] I am not suggesting that the motives of Fields, Scudder, or others in this establishment were narrowly mercenary or baldly political. They were sincere (assuming one trusts the evidence and finds the category meaningful), and they succeeded in making particular kinds of literary achievement possible. Rather, I am suggesting that the literary distinction they championed was founded on paradoxes that grew more vexing as the publishing industry expanded and social divisions sharpened. At one and the same time, it disclaimed commercial motives and constituted a market. It affirmed a cultural hierarchy that both legitimized and depended upon a social hierarchy widely felt, by the end of the nineteenth century, to be rather precarious. Within that framework, writing could be – shall I say, accomplished and apprehended? or produced and consumed? These are not simple questions; indeed, the writings of Howells and James, who inherited and extended the project of writing and selling distinguished literature, can be taken as extended meditations on the mysteries of this traffic in words.

The realm of undistinguished writing against which fine literature was defined was frequently characterized as feminine. Many readers in the midcentury's growing market for fiction were women, and many writers who cultivated it were women; feminist criticism has recently recovered a whole group of authors who for most of the twentieth century figured in literary history only as Hawthorne's "damn'd mob of scribbling women." Precisely what elite publishing attempted to constitute was a scene of reading and a source of value that escaped domesticity, that subsumed but was not confined to or dependent on that sphere; it reacted, as later revisionings of American literature do, against the "feminization" of American cultural life.[28]

But no simple equivalence between female and popular, male and elite culture should be assumed. From its beginnings genteel literary culture certainly addressed women as readers, and it included them, less certainly, as writers; Harriet Beecher Stowe and Rose Terry Cooke were among the thirteen contributors to the first issue of the *Atlantic Monthly* in 1857. Jewett was welcomed into genteel literary culture and, although there are generational distinctions to be drawn, affiliated herself with it. Spending her winters from 1882 on with Annie Fields at 148 Charles Street put her close to its heart. Nevertheless, the available positions in this cultural system are marked by gender, and the conjunction of "literary distinction" and "female author" is an intrinsically uneasy one. The rich confusions and controversies over Stowe, who had the strongest claim to be considered a great writer, indicate how difficult a crux this is; even now proposals for revising our understanding of nineteenth-century American literature seem, with striking frequency, to entail new suggestions about where in the tradition she might fit.[29]

As Mary Kelley has shown, the paradox of the popular women writers of the midcentury was that they participated in the marketplace by writing about the home, entering the public forum as private women; they were, in her phrase, "literary domestics."[30] Annie Fields's very different, but equally literary and domestic life tells us much about how women participated in elite literary culture. It is not so much that her biography lets us glimpse some of the private underpinnings of the milieu that do not figure in loftier accounts — we see how much time and effort went into her entertaining (and what that cost in terms of her own serious literary aspirations), her disapproval of the way some of the men in her circle treated their wives, the petty feuds among the literati.[31] We also see Fields as a partner in her husband's enterprises, not only playing a crucial role as a hostess in a house paid for by the firm, but reading and evaluating submissions, editing manuscripts, and handling correspondence. (A number of writers, particularly women, wrote to Annie and James jointly or simply to Annie.) As one critic observes, "A gifted woman in a position of power, she managed to develop her talents and exert her influence without violating propriety."[32] The terms of her success and her subordination imply each other; the paradox for Annie Fields was that, having entered literary culture specifically as a wife, she was a far more important actor than could be publicly acknowledged.

Annie Fields wielded power in two arenas: a masculine publishing establishment and a "female world" of literary friendships. In effect, she mediated between them. (Josephine Donovan goes so far as to suggest that the New England local-color movement could not have existed without her.)[33] Fields exchanged letters with notable women, from Jane Addams and Rose Terry Cooke to Christina Rossetti and Frances Willard. Her biographer offers a partial list of her correspondents almost fifty names long, writing:

> Fields is generally acknowledged to have been at the center of a loosely knit circle of women writers that not only included New England writers but also extended well into what is now the Midwest. Although many of these writers never met, and even those who lived relatively close to each other seldom had the time or the means to visit each other, they supported each other with letters full of encouragement. They exchanged photographs, manuscripts, and published books. They congratulated each other on marriages and children and consoled each other on the deaths of family members. They understood, as most of the male writers did not, the difficulties that women faced when they tried to achieve distinction in the arts. In addition to writers, the support network included women painters, sculptors, stained-glass artists, educators, reformers, actresses, and others. The network was international as well, including English and a few French women.[34]

Jewett was a member of this circle in her own right, as well as through her connection with Fields; she corresponded with most of the important female authors of her time, including Stowe, Cooke, Julia Ward Howe, Elizabeth Stuart Phelps Ward, Mary Wilkins Freeman, Helen Hunt Jackson, and others.

Jewett and Fields had an inner circle of friends in New England as well. The members of this close community were for the most part active participants in elite cultural life, although they are now considered only minor figures: the poet Celia Thaxter, for example, and the artist Sarah Wyman Whitman. Sara Norton, to whom Jewett wrote about the transfiguring qualities of friendship, was a cellist (and the sister of the influential Harvard scholar and author Charles Eliot Norton). Alice Greenwood Howe, to whom Jewett dedicated *The Country of the Pointed Firs*, was one of the founders of the Boston Symphony Orchestra. Fields herself was engaged in philanthropy and reform, in addition to poetry writing, literary editing, and translating. The feminist critics who have delineated this community have shown that it also comprised a female literary tradition. Its participants shared a knowledge of, and a high value for, a whole body of works by women – including writers distant in time and place, as well as predecessors like Stowe who were personally known to them and contemporaries. Reading Jewett's work as part of a strong, well-established and still-developing female literary tradition has made it possible to understand it in ways that depart radically from dominant twentieth-century interpretations, as we will see. It also helps us to understand why friendship and literary influence blend so seamlessly for Jewett; as her letters clearly show, when moved by a literary work, she responded by expressing a sense of connection with, and gratitude to, the author and a desire to share the experience with a friend.[35] Jewett felt profoundly at home in the world of literature.

Knowledge of the female tradition serves as a corrective to literary historians' earlier views of the nineteenth century; but the fact that we encounter two separate bodies of literary criticism should not mislead us into thinking that the literary culture they describe was so thoroughly segregated. Jewett loved and was influenced by Flaubert as well as Austen, Tennyson as well as Stowe; her intimate friends included John Greenleaf Whittier and Thomas Bailey Aldrich.[36] By Jewett's day, too, middle-class women's expectations of participating in public life had increased. One might take as emblematic the fact that although the gentlemen contributors to the *Atlantic Monthly* had long gathered for dinners, when in 1877 owner Henry Houghton organized a more formal celebration on the occasion of Whittier's seventieth, and the magazine's twentieth, birthday the women protested their exclusion. (The publicity surrounding the event, and the fact that Whittier was closely connected with so many literary women, no doubt increased their indignation.) The women of the *Atlantic Monthly*, Jewett among them, were invited to and attended the celebration of Holmes's seventieth birthday in 1879; a newspaper account called their inclusion "a new departure – a historical event, an innovation of a startling and a very important character."[37] The next such occasion, in 1882, honored Harriet Beecher Stowe.

The first issue of the *Atlantic Monthly* dealt with many topics, from Florentine mosaics to finance, but both Stowe and Cooke contributed New England sketches.[38] The place accorded to women writers in "quality" literature was above all that of recorders of regional life. Eric Sundquist indicates the importance of such writing at this historical moment when he points out that Jewett's work is

> representative of a paradoxical effect of much local color writing, namely, that the same communication and transportation developments that closed the nation's sectional divisions following the Civil War and brought isolated communities closer also began to destroy rural "islands" of life. Local color records in part the rustic border world rendered exotic by industrialism but now made visible and nostalgically charged by the nation's inexorable drive toward cohesion and standardization.[39]

Among the writers of local-color fiction throughout the nation, one finds a strong representation of women and people of color; their accounts were accorded legitimacy.[40] But the very terms in which they were included in the tradition ensured their subordination. As Raymond Williams wrote of the English novel some time ago, it was

> as a function of increasingly centralized states . . . that "region" came to take on its modern meaning of "a subordinate area", a sense which is of course compatible with recognition of its now "local" – "regional" – characteristics.
>
> And then what is striking, in matters of cultural description, is the steady discrimination of certain regions as in this limited sense "regional", which can only hold if certain other regions are not seen in this way. . . . [T]his is no longer a distinction of areas and kinds of

life; it is what is politely called a value-judgement but more accurately an expression of centralized cultural dominance.[41]

The genre of Jewett's work itself entails James's sense that it is "of minor compass," although I will suggest later that she implicitly challenges the limits that come with this territory.

New England was the site of the strongest and most definitely female-dominated movement; and in a period when population and economic growth, as well as cultural and political dominance, were shifting elsewhere, the region itself seems to have been feminized. Literary historians uniformly cite this historical context and reproduce the characterization of the local colorists as nostalgic documentarists. Perry Westbrook writes in *Acres of Flint*, originally published in 1951 and recently reprinted, "There are . . . many fully qualified 'recorders of the New England decline,' as Fred Pattee has called them. Some of them, such as Mary Wilkins Freeman and Sarah Orne Jewett, are important, if not major, figures in American letters. . . . [T]hey give a detailed and accurate contemporary picture of New England during the times of stress." Westbrook does, however, question Jewett's ability to assess what she sees, finding for example her character Captain Littlepage "a pitiful, deranged old man. But Miss Jewett sets him up as a typical sea-captain of the old school. . . . Miss Jewett is perfectly sincere; she is simply seeing in the Captain more than was ever there."[42] An emphasis on the oddity of the characters is characteristic of this view of local color. The author of the article "Regionalism" in the 1988 *Columbia Literary History of the United States* writes that Jewett, Freeman, and Brown portray "the isolate individual at the edge of eccentricity" and repeats the assertion that New England itself was lacking: the local-color writers "gave one last cultivation to the region, but it is a region whose nature has grown thin, whose economy has grown stingy, whose society has grown small."[43] The persistent reader of Jewett criticism comes to feel, in the words of the narrator of *The Country of the Pointed Firs* as she ends a conversation with Captain Littlepage, that she is "familiar with the subject of the decadence of shipping interests in all its affecting branches"[44] — indeed, somewhat too familiar.

As Michael Bell points out in Chapter 3 of this volume, the

17

aspirations of local-color fiction to "tell [people and things] just as they are," as Jewett's father advised her to do, ally it with literary realism.[45] But there was also considerable tension among the stances of these movements. As Bell goes on to show, in the 1880s and later Howells and other embattled proponents of varieties of realism were striving to masculinize literature, explicitly distancing themselves from genteel culture and envisioning fiction writing as a vocation to grapple with the strenuous facts of contemporary American life. Jewett was as confident as any realist that writing was her work in the world. Certainly she never appealed, as the literary domestics did, to financial necessity or the need for moral literature to justify publishing; she did hope to be "useful."[46] Her fictional practice seems to accommodate both genteel and realist imperatives: it achieves both elegant style and apparently transparent representation; explicitly didactic only on rare occasions, it is nevertheless pervaded by a strong moral sense and a strong spiritual sensibility (each distinctively Christian if not necessarily orthodox).[47] And like her fictional practice, Jewett's expressed views on writing are a complex amalgam; she accords places to both accuracy and the imagination, to both an Arnoldian view of culture as "the best that has been thought and said" and an uncompromising openness to everyday truth and common life.[48]

This compound of ideas, combined with her deep sense of a personal relationship to literary tradition and her financial independence (due to an inheritance from her grandfather), allowed Jewett to take an extraordinarily confident stance toward her own place in the traffic of words. This serenity has been mistaken for simplicity, and the complexity of Jewett's view of authorship has been lost in the general tendency to treat women's writings as unselfconscious emanations and the specific belief that the female local colorists were stenographers of simple lives. Thus Howells compared her to a thrush. Kipling expressed the mingled respect and depreciation that have become familiar, writing to Jewett of *The Country of the Pointed Firs* that her " 'perfect little tale' " is " 'immense' " and (as Annie Fields reported) adding "jovially in the postscript, 'I don't believe even you know how good that work is.' "[49] Later, Van Wyck Brooks not only declared that Jewett's vision was limited, but wrote about her without making a distinction between art and life; he asserts as simple fact that Jewett rented a schoolhouse to work in while on vacation in Maine, although there is no evidence for it beyond the fact that the narrator of *The Country of the Pointed Firs* does so (in fact, it is virtually certain that Jewett did not).[50] In a 1954 book asserting the seriousness and value of the American realist movement, Everett Carter called the novel a collection of "etchings of New England life" in which "the transition from fiction to nonfiction is so slight as to be imperceptible."[51] Many other examples could be cited. Jewett's work is responsible enough to the historical circumstances out of which it was written to be useful for historians – Laurel Ulrich finds it a valuable source for her remarkable *Midwife's Tale*, for example.[52] But saying that it can enter into a complex adequation of sources of historical evidence is very different from saying that it simply tells the truth.

The center of gravity in the interpretation of American literature shifted decisively, after the First World War, to colleges and universities. Courses in American literature were taught sporadically from the last quarter of the nineteenth century on, and of course nonacademic reviewers and readers continue to exert influence; but both the expansion of higher education and enthusiastic postwar Americanism led to greatly increased professional attention to American literature.[53] As studies of the politics of canon formation in the twentieth century have shown, the local-color writers, and in fact most women and nonwhite writers who in 1920 were thought worthy of inclusion in anthologies and course syllabi, had been eliminated from them by 1950. Those who participated in this process often disagree with one another; both Arnoldian humanists critical of professionalization and research-oriented philologists promoting it used gendered and racialized rhetoric. The mechanisms through which it worked were complex, ranging from outright misogyny expressed in essays like "The Feminine Nuisance in American Literature" and the creation of theories of the nature of American literature that simply defined away the concerns of women writers, to the reorganization of the Modern Language Association.[54] The cumulative result was another, very successful masculinization of cultural work. Jewett held onto a small place in literary history. But despite the praise always given

19

to her style, she was not even mentioned in Richard Poirier's influential *A World Elsewhere: The Place of Style in American Literature*, published in 1966.[55]

Sharon O'Brien's examination of how Willa Cather was demoted from a "major" to a "minor" writer is not only a model study in the politics of twentieth-century canon formation, but casts light in passing on the decline of Jewett's reputation and Cather's attempt to retrieve it. When in 1925 Cather edited Jewett for Houghton Mifflin, O'Brien reports, she "was determined to increase Jewett's size, literally and figuratively. She told editor Ferris Greenslet that the existing editions of Jewett's fiction were simply too small – people would refuse to take them out of libraries, she explained, because they would assume they were children's books. Greenslet promised her an edition in a larger format, and in her introduction Cather addressed her real aim – increasing Jewett's literary stature" (with, in part, the words I quoted early in this chapter). Her essay on Jewett in *Not Under Forty* reflected her continuing distress at "dismissals of Jewett as a minor writer whose spinsterish eccentricity and genteel prudishness prevented her from addressing important subjects"; it was a losing battle, and she diminished her claims for her mentor in the 1936 volume. The negative reviews it received silenced her.[56]

The version of *The Country of the Pointed Firs* printed in Cather's edition was enlarged in another sense as well. When Houghton Mifflin published it as part of a seven-volume edition of Jewett's work in 1910, a year after her death, two later Dunnet Landing stories ("A Dunnet Shepherdess" and the unfinished "William's Wedding") were interpolated between the penultimate and the final chapter; in 1919 "The Queen's Twin" was added at the end of the novel. These decisions seem to have been somewhat casual; an uncollected Dunnet story now considered among Jewett's finest, "The Foreigner," was not included, and the order settled on violated chronology more than was necessary.[57] Cather accepted the additions, although she did not originate them. By the standards of modern textual scholarship, this was a rather outrageous alteration. It presumably did not seem so to those involved; Jewett was in the habit of forming collections out of published stories and had added chapters to the book between its serial and book publication. Moreover, everyone, including Jewett herself, agreed that plot construction was not one of her strengths. But the reader of *The Country of the Pointed Firs* today will prefer to read the novel Jewett wrote and is well advised to examine the text in hand carefully to be sure that it has twenty-one chapters. The later Dunnet stories ought, certainly, to be read, but as separate texts.

Reading Jewett as part of a female literary tradition has made it possible to show that the novel does, indeed, have an integral shape that is violated by interpolations. Feminist critics have argued that what we see is not so much an inability to create traditional plots as the creation of an alternative way of narrating female experience. Elizabeth Ammons, one of the contributors to this volume, has proposed (in an earlier essay) a reading of *The Country of the Pointed Firs* as structured by two interdependent patterns. One is linear; the narrator moves from solitary absorption in the business of writing to an understanding of and participation in the community. The other pattern, less conventional and more important, is radial, a network in which the narrative "constantly moves out from its base to a given point and back again, out to another point and back again, out again, back again, and so forth, like arteries on a spider web."[58] The spatial center of this web is Mrs. Todd's home in Dunnet Landing; its dramatic center is the home of Mrs. Blackett, Mrs. Todd's mother, on Green Island – particularly the pennyroyal grove there, which takes on virtually sacred significance. In this structure, Ammons argues, relationships accumulate (as in the networks of friendship Smith-Rosenberg describes) rather than compete with one another. Another contributor to this volume, Sandra Zagarell, has complemented this view by analyzing *The Country of the Pointed Firs* in terms of a genre she calls the "narrative of community." She argues persuasively for the existence of a whole group of works, written primarily by women, that disregard linear development to offer an episodically structured portrait of daily collective life and give "literary expression to a community they imagine to have characterized the preindustrial era."[59]

Marcia McClintock Folsom's influential essay on Jewett's "empathic style" is another illuminating reading of the form of *The Country of the Pointed Firs* – again, in terms of innovation rather than lack. This style, in Folsom's account, relies heavily upon the interweaving of narration and dialogue (Folsom does not cite Bahktin, but she could have). It also relies upon dramatizing cognition; Folsom finds the key to Jewett's method in a key passage from the Green Island sequence: "Tact is after all a kind of mind-reading, and my hostess held the golden gift. Sympathy is of the mind as well as the heart" (p. 46). Jewett has links to the philosophical and literary tradition of sentimentality in which right action springs from right feeling, but she carefully demonstrates that achieving mutual understanding and reciprocal affection requires "intelligent curiosity, mental activity, specific knowledge" as well. Through close textual analysis, Folsom shows how the novel offers the reader the opportunity to participate in the process by which the narrator and Mrs. Todd observe details and make deductions from them to reconstruct their social meaning. "Different in their knowledge of Dunnet Landing, the two women are alike in their impulse to see into and beyond casual conversation, gesture, and expression, or details of houses, weather, and landscape, to identify the larger human significance of each small outer sign." And as Folsom recognizes, successful empathy also requires the "accessibility of the natural and social world to reliable interpretation. The narrator's extraordinary responsiveness to what she sees and hears is the corollary of the expressiveness of the world in Jewett's work."[60] Some critics have suggested that Jewett's world lacks conflict, which is demonstrably untrue; but it is never unintelligible. Elizabeth Ammons's essay in this volume carries forward this analysis, examining the legibility of material culture in *The Country of the Pointed Firs*.

Ammons, Zagarell, and Folsom have articulated how the form of *The Country of the Pointed Firs* works on sympathetic readers; they have given an account of the elusive power of Jewett's fiction to seem "immense" even to some of those who automatically categorize it as "little." These as well as thematic insights, such as Sarah Way Sherman's illuminating examination of Jewett's sources in classical literature and scholarship,[61] have derived from reading Jewett in terms of women's concerns, locating her in what Josephine Donovan calls "the world of the mothers."[62] But we should also note Margaret Roman's suggestion that Jewett "consciously collapses gender dichotomies. She, in effect, dissolves the binary oppositions of gender, of the polarities termed woman and man."[63] Michael Bell, in Chapter 3 of this volume, addresses the tension implied here; as he suggests, Jewett makes both affirmation of women and resistance to women's condition available though not explicit. As Denise Riley and Nancy Cott, among others, have shown, that tension is constitutive for feminism; advocacy for women bases itself on sex solidarity even as it strives to defeat a prescriptive unity, and both arguments based on sexual difference and on equality or sameness are indispensable.[64] In this Jewett proves to be a writer not only of her own moment, but of a long moment we share with her.

One must resist the temptation of an ahistorical affirmation of continuity, however; as Susan Gillman points out in Chapter 5 of this volume, feminist criticism of Jewett has tended to emphasize "difference" arguments and essentialize female identity. The essays by Sandra Zagarell and Elizabeth Ammons (Chapters 2 and 4) offer significant rereadings of their previous work, examining the ways in which the community of *The Country of the Pointed Firs* is racialized and nationalist, even imperialist. The essays published here combine the insights of feminist readings of Jewett with the new analysis of regionalism that has emerged in the past few years in the work of Sundquist, Brodhead, Philip Fisher, and Amy Kaplan. The volume constitutes a dialogue rather than a consensus, but its remarkably cohesive collective project is to produce a historicized reading of Jewett in terms of gender, genre, region, and nation.

The received view of regionalism in American literary history has emphasized its effort to render the local and conserve the traditional, rather than the way in which the impulse to do so is dependent on and part of a drive toward national unification. The "invention of tradition" is a distinctively modern activity; local-color fiction, in the broadest perspective, forms part of the great wave of such efforts in Europe and the United States from about 1870 to the First World War.[65] Amy Kaplan, using Jewett as her primary example, argues that the "decentralization of literature contributes to solidifying national centrality by reimagining a distended industrial nation as an extended clan sharing a 'common inheritance' in its imagined rural origins." On the one hand, she suggests, regionalism "expands the boundaries of the imagined community and democratizes access to literary representation." On the other, it

> contained the threatening conflicts of social difference, just as dialect itself bracketed the speaker as uneducated and inferior to the urban narrator with his standard English. This hierarchy structured the conditions of literary production for regionalist writers as well, who were published by a highly centralized industry located in Boston and New York that appealed to an urban middle-class readership; this readership was solidified as an imagined community by consuming images of rural "others" as both a nostagic point of origin and a measure of cosmopolitan development.[66]

Kaplan, although less affirmative than Alice Brown was about that "national being" in which the pointed firs have their roots, has returned to her insight about the novel. Susan Gillman's essay reacts to and develops these insights, supporting the argument that local-color fiction in general, and Jewett's in particular, is deeply engaged in the continuing project of creating a national culture.

Kaplan's view of this body of fiction as "literary tourism" is precisely the opposite of that proposed by two feminist critics who have recently edited a Norton anthology called *American Women Regionalists*. Judith Fetterley and Marjorie Pryse acknowledge that they are suggesting a view different from that of the writers themselves, but suggest that rather than treating local color as a movement that can be subsumed into the larger category of regionalism, we see the two as quite different forms: "The regionalist narrator empowers the voice of regional characters, viewing them as agents of their own lives, rather than undermining them with the ironic perspective characteristic of 'local color' writing."[67] For many readers of Jewett's work, this rings true; Folsom's work on "empathetic style" suggests how, at the level of the sentence, narrative might evoke such a sense of agency. Kaplan too acknowledges that *The Country of the Pointed Firs* "cedes to the local the authority to define itself through its vernacular history, conversation, natural rhythms." But the derogatory comments about Jewett and the dull old ladies who inhabit her fiction to be found in the record of interpretations – even the limited sample given in this essay –

make it amply clear that the "empathetic style" cannot enforce a proper attitude upon any given reader. I would argue that Fetterley and Pryse's view of regionalism is untenable because it makes the definition of the genre depend upon its *effect*, and unhelpful because their analytic claim translates so rapidly into an evaluative one.

Jewett's own statements about her fiction seem to support both sides of this debate. She saw herself as a kind of advocate for her characters:

> When I was, perhaps, fifteen, the first "city boarders" began to make their appearance near Berwick; and the way they misconstrued the country people and made game of their peculiarities fired me with indignation. I determined to teach the world that country people were not the awkward, ignorant set those people seemed to think. I wanted the world to know their grand, simple lives; and, so far as I had a mission, when I first began to write, I think that was it.[68]

But the adjectives "grand" and "simple" remind us that Jewett necessarily construes characters through her own frameworks – and the essays in this volume provide a great deal of new information about Jewett's frameworks. Kaplan is right, I believe, in observing that *The Country of the Pointed Firs* often represents country folk as premodern, even childlike, repositories of value, "both outside history and at the origin of history"; as Susan Gillman shows, Jewett projects difference along both spatial and chronological axes. But neither empathy nor literary tourism defines a genre; rather, both are necessary possibilities in a literary form that dramatizes and itself enacts connections between locations in a centralizing political and cultural economy.

Jewett certainly does, as the received view of regionalism would suggest, strive to convey the particular qualities of rural New England life. This aspect of her work is effectively evoked by a frequently quoted passage in "From a Mournful Villager": "People do not know what they lose when they make way with the reserve, the separateness, the sanctity of the front yard of their grandmothers. . . . [W]e Americans had better build more fences than take any away from our lives" (p. 127). Jay Martin writes that Jewett built a "fictive fence" around her birthplace, and Marilyn

25

Sanders Mobley uses the image to frame one of the chapters in her book on the "folk roots" of Jewett's and Toni Morrison's work.[69] Fetterley and Pryse understand the region as a separate, bounded site of meaning when they write, "Characters in regional fiction are rooted; they don't leave home in search of their identity."[70] But Jewett's characters are very often in motion, and when stationary they are often busy reacting to someone's arrival or departure. For example, the other pieces that make up *Country By-Ways*, in which "From a Mournful Villager" appears, are four sketches that follow journeys by boat, on horseback, on foot, and by carriage; and three stories that narrate the circumstances of one man's emigration to Boston, a family's first visit to what will become their beloved summer home in the country, and the "pilgrimage" of a woman who returns from western New York to her birthplace in New England. From the multiple long-distance visits embedded in her first *Atlantic Monthly* story, "Mr. Bruce" (1869), to the country ramble and supernatural messages of "The Green Bowl" (1901), and at all points between, Jewett is deeply and systematically concerned with circuits of communication and transportation.

Jewett in fact depicts a very complex transformation in *The Country of the Pointed Firs*, one that is obscured if her work is assimilated too quickly to a narrative of decline or of progress toward national integration. She describes a shift from a system of global interconnections through shipping to one in which the relationship between the village and other parts of the world is mediated by the metropolis. Captain Littlepage laments: "A community narrows down and grows dreadful ignorant when it is shut up to its own affairs, and gets no knowledge of the outside world except from a cheap, unprincipled newspaper. In the old days, a good part o' the best men here knew a hundred ports and something of the way folks lived in them. They saw the world for themselves, and like's not their wives and children saw it with them" (p. 20). Jewett's stories include treatments of many phenomena associated with a modernizing America: the influence of journalism, factory layoffs, the rise of tourism, the relations between native-born Americans and immigrants.[71] Even when not addressing such topics, her work is infused with a vivid experience of locality and a

26

powerful sense of interconnectedness; each must be achieved, but they do not undermine each other. Jewett is a sophisticated, and unusually optimistic, analyst of what Anthony Giddens describes as one of the constitutive features of modernity: "the complex relations between *local involvements* (circumstances of co-presence) and *interaction across distance* (the connections of presence and absence)."[72]

We see Jewett's concern with interaction across distance in the fact that the railroad is a constant presence in her fiction. One might think of Miss Catherine Spring, in the 1878 story "A Late Supper," as a New England spinster living quietly behind a fictive fence. But she is failing to make ends meet because of "the failure of a certain railway to pay its dividend" and because her advertisement for summer boarders in a Boston newspaper has gone unanswered. The story turns on her generosity in giving cakes and all the cream she has to a little girl who has come asking for work because of the hard times (the reference to the depression that had begun in 1873 would have been obvious to contemporary readers). Unexpected guests come to tea, and Miss Spring makes a hasty journey down the road to borrow cream from a neighbor; while returning she mounts the platform to cross a train standing on the tracks and blocking her way – and is carried off, "cream-pitcher and all, without a bit of a bonnet."[73] Two empathetic ladies take her into their compartment, pay her fare, loan her a hood, and wrap her pitcher respectably in paper. Eventually they come back to take the rooms Miss Spring wishes to rent. "A Late Supper" focuses intensely on a small number of subjective states and face-to-face interactions to realize a vivid sense of *place*, in Giddens's sense of a geographically specific site of social activity.[74] Yet it also addresses the impact of distant decisions and events on local life; indeed, the locomotive on which Miss Spring finds herself riding – exclaiming, " 'I wish we never had sold our land for the track! Oh! what shall I do?' " (p. 95) – can be taken as a figure for the immense forces of modernity. (It was used as such by other authors of the period.) But for Jewett, this rupture serves as an opening for a happy ending, as human kindness intervenes. The connectedness that concerns Jewett is at once economic, social, and spiritual: Her adventure on the train solves Miss Spring's fi-

27

nancial difficulties, enriches her life with new friends, and demonstrates the providential ordering of things; the change allows her to take in the little girl, a decision in which the hiring of help, an act of charity, and adoption are conflated.

The Country of the Pointed Firs too is concerned with presence and absence, juxtaposing "local involvements" and "interactions across distance." It vividly affirms the possibility of human connection across time and space in the "golden chain of love and dependence" (p. 90) that unites Mrs. Blackett on her remote island with her family and friends and weaves even the reclusive Joanna into an inclusive, empathetic fellowship of the cell (p. 82). Devotion overcomes even greater divisions – of time, space, and social position – in "Martha's Lady" and the late Dunnet Landing story "The Queen's Twin." Feminist critics have treated these stories as celebrations of bonds between women. Yet discussion of a story about the love of a maid for a lady, expressed through perfect service in a house her idol visited once, ought surely also to address questions of inequality and subordination.[75] Jewett shows spiritual beauty in a life devoutly spent in what Ann Romines calls "domestic ritual" – housekeeping – but the order she depicts, like nineteenth-century improvements in manners as John Kasson has displayed them, implies not only civility but hierarchy.[76] And what are we to make of a poor, rural Maine widow's feeling of identification and companionship with Queen Victoria, however successfully Jewett renders the rich subjective meaning that sense of connection holds? It has too rarely been said that Jewett uniformly assumes the benevolence of authority. Yet it would be wrong to ignore the fact that, like Henry James, Jewett implies a virtually utopian "conception of possibilities of relation" among human beings. I use James's phrase for James Fields's vision of a new kind of publishing house deliberately, for such possibilities are necessarily thought *through* existing social arrangements – they are articulated as part of our traffic in words. Like other Arnoldians, Jewett is both profoundly democratic in envisioning universal participation in culture and profoundly antidemocratic in what she imagines culture to be.

In similarly paradoxical fashion, Jewett works in a form that is constituted by its subordinate relationship to national culture, yet embeds in her fiction a radical rejection of the hierarchy of region. She writes in the opening of "A Late Supper": "One never hears much about Brookton when one is away from it, but, for all that, life is as important and exciting there as it is anywhere" (p. 80). For Jewett, as this passage suggests, one finds the center of the world is not on the site of social dominance, but on the site of consciousness; it is potentially everywhere and anywhere. (This refusal of arrangements of subordination is evoked, indirectly, in Louis Renza's argument that Jewett systematically chooses to write "minor" literature.)[77] She is committed to what Charles Taylor calls the "affirmation of ordinary life." From this perspective, the "highest life can no longer be defined by an exalted *kind* of activity; it all turns on the *spirit* in which one lives whatever one lives, even the most mundane existence."[78] In Jewett's fiction this claim is ontological rather than explicitly religious. (The glancing allusion of the title – not the last, but a late, supper – is characteristic.) But we will, I suspect, more fully understand Jewett's articulation of the local, the national, and the putatively universal when we confront her view of democracy as rooted in spiritual sources.

Jewett's sense of the value of ordinary life is also, it seems to me, linked to her refusal to be difficult. She persists in finding significance immanent in everyday surfaces, never making the reordering of perception a necessity for apprehending her writing as some other writers – James, for example – begin to do in this period; her apparently transparent narration makes itself available for a very wide variety of interpretations. She requires that we pay attention to the local, to the density and intimacy of face-to-face interaction, in order to apprehend how other solidarities are woven and what they mean. Those so inclined can belittle her work; it does not proclaim its bigness in the strenuous, masculine terms of other versions of the imagined community of America at the turn into the twentieth century.[79] Yet even in the face of the forces that relentlessly define her concerns and characters as marginal, the experience of reading *The Country of the Pointed Firs* has, for many readers, sustained a sense that Dunnet Landing's "childish certainty of being the centre of civilization" (p. 2) embodies a complex corrective to the pretensions of the metropolis.

Jewett's affirmation of the ordinary life of ordinary people, as the essays that follow amply demonstrate, can never disengage from the historical conditions of possibility in which it emerges. Walter Benjamin said this in one way: "There is no document of civilization which is not at the same time a document of barbarism."[80] Willa Cather, proved wrong by events in her assertion that *The Country of the Pointed Firs* could "confront time and change securely" but unwilling to abandon wholly her claims for Jewett, said it in another: "To note an artist's limitations is but to define his talent."[81] The book we examine here is not a timeless masterpiece. It is precisely because this is a moment when women reading as women are prominent in literary scholarship, and when the construction of racialized nationality has assumed a new significance and urgency in our thinking, that Jewett's work is more legible now than just a few years ago. *The Country of the Pointed Firs* appears today as fully the equal in craft and resonant substance of the novels to which Cather compared it and as one of the most rewardingly complex American narratives we have.

NOTES

I wish to thank Michael Bell, Susan Gillman, Ira Sadoff, Diane Sampson, and especially David Scobey for their assistance with this essay.

1. Willa Cather, Preface to *The Best Short Stories of Sarah Orne Jewett*, 2 vols. (Boston: Houghton Mifflin, 1925), vol. 1., p. xix.
2. Alice Brown, originally published in *Book Buyer* (1897); rpt. in Gwen L. Nagel, ed., *Critical Essays on Sarah Orne Jewett* (Boston: Hall, 1984), pp. 37–9.
3. Anon., *Bookman* (New York), 5 (1897): 80–1.
4. For a summary of contemporary reviews see Gwen L. Nagel and James Nagel, *Sarah Orne Jewett: A Reference Guide* (Boston: Hall, 1978). Quoted phrases can be found on p. 32.
5. Henry James, "Mr. and Mrs. Fields," originally published in *Cornhill Magazine* (England) and *Atlantic Monthly*, 1915; rpt. in Henry James, *The American Essays*, ed. Leon Edel (1956; Princeton, N.J.: Princeton Univ. Press, 1989), p. 278.

6. The Jewetts had particularly strong links to Exeter (site of Phillips Exeter Academy and home of Jewett's maternal grandfather, a famous surgeon; Jewett was connected with the Gilmans, the leading family of the town, through her grandmother) and Brunswick (where her father held an appointment in the medical school at Bowdoin College).

7. Some years ago the house was painstakingly restored to its appearance in the latter part of Jewett's life, and it is now open to the public. See Martha Ackmann, "Guide to American Women Writers' Homes, Part 2," *Legacy* 2, no. 1 (1985): 11.

8. Sarah Orne Jewett, *Country By-Ways* (1881; rpt. Freeport, N.Y.: Books for Libraries Press, 1969).

9. For biographical information I rely on John Eldridge Frost, *Sarah Orne Jewett* (Kittery Point, Me.: Gundalow Club, 1960), Sarah Way Sherman, *Sarah Orne Jewett, an American Persephone* (Hanover, N.H.: Univ. Press of New England, 1989) (see Sherman, especially, for comments on Jewett's relationship with her mother and on female friendship), and the Chronology in Michael Bell's forthcoming edition of Jewett for the Library of America. See also Francis Otto Matthiessen, *Sarah Orne Jewett* (Boston: Houghton Mifflin, 1929).

10. Frost, *Sarah Orne Jewett*, 49.

11. Carroll Smith-Rosenberg, "The Female World of Love and Ritual," in *Disorderly Conduct: Visions of Gender in Victorian America* (New York: Oxford Univ. Press, 1985), quotations from pp. 60, 73, 63, 53, and 61–2. The thirty-five families from which Smith-Rosenberg draws her evidence are all members of the literate, white middle class, although their regional, religious, and economic circumstances vary; her study is clearly relevant to, if not beyond, Jewett's milieu.

12. Karen Lystra, *Searching the Heart: Women, Men, and Romantic Love in Nineteenth-Century America* (New York: Oxford Univ. Press, 1989), addresses this point.

13. Willa Cather, *Not Under Forty* (New York: Knopf, 1936), p. 85.

14. Annie Fields, ed., *Letters of Sarah Orne Jewett* (Boston: Houghton Mifflin, 1911), p. 126.

15. Elizabeth Ammons, "Jewett's Witches," in Nagel, ed., *Critical Essays*, pp. 165–84.

16. Sharon O'Brien, " 'The Thing Not Named': Willa Cather as a Lesbian Writer," *Signs* 9, no. 4 (1984): 591.

17. Fields, ed., *Letters*, pp. 246–7.

18. Mark Anthony DeWolfe Howe's influence is detailed by Josephine

Donovan in "The Unpublished Love Poems of Sarah Orne Jewett," in Nagel, ed., *Critical Essays*, pp. 107–17. Donovan argues the case for considering Jewett as a lesbian writer.

19. Richard Brodhead, *The School of Hawthorne* (New York: Oxford Univ. Press, 1986), 59. Although the fact does not affect the point I am making here, Jewett's friendship with Scudder cooled after about 1890; see Margaret Roman, *Sarah Orne Jewett: Reconstructing Gender* (Tuscaloosa: Univ. of Alabama Press, 1992), pp. 121–2.

20. James, *American Essays*, p. 266.

21. Brodhead, *School of Hawthorne*, pp. 54–5.

22. Cather, *Not Under Forty*, pp. 56–7. Salvini, Modjeska, Booth, and Jefferson were actors, Bull a violinist, Nilsson a soprano – all among the best-known performers of their day.

23. A historian of our own day, John Tebbel, still adopts this view when he writes, "To see the imprint of the Riverside Press on a book, and its familiar motto, 'Do It Well, or Not At All,' was a guarantee of excellence, not only in printing, for which the press was famous, but of literary superiority" (*A History of Book Publishing in the United States*, vol. 2: *The Expansion of an Industry, 1865–1919*, [New York: Bowker, 1975), p. 253). There are battered "Riverside Editions" from my own college courses on my shelf. The series was discontinued for some time but has been revived; it currently includes Hawthorne, Howells, James, Arnold, Austen, Tennyson, Thackeray, and Flaubert, but not Jewett (so far, at least).

24. Brodhead, *School of Hawthorne*, p. 59.

25. Matthew Arnold, *Culture and Anarchy* (1869), ed. J. Dover Wilson (New York: Cambridge Univ. Press, 1932), p. 46. Zagarell comments on the direct relationship between Arnold and Jewett in Chapter 2 of this volume.

26. See Lawrence Levine, *Highbrow/Lowbrow: The Emergence of Cultural Hierarchy in America* (Cambridge, Mass.: Harvard Univ. Press, 1988); see also John Kasson, *Rudeness and Civility: Manners in Nineteenth-Century America* (New York: Hall & Wang; Farrar Straus & Giroux, 1990), esp. chap. 7, "The Disciplining of Spectatorship."

27. Brodhead, *School of Hawthorne*, p. 56.

28. The phrase is that of Ann Douglas, *The Feminization of American Culture* (New York: Knopf, 1977).

29. Ann Douglas, *The Feminization of American Culture*, and Jane Tompkins, *Sensational Designs: The Cultural Work of American Fiction, 1790–1860* (New York: Oxford Univ. Press, 1985), make Stowe central to arguments about the nature of sentimental fiction; Nina Baym

excludes her from the tradition in *Woman's Fiction: A Guide to Novels by and about Women in America, 1820–1870* (Ithaca, N.Y.: Cornell Univ. Press, 1978); Josephine Donovan, *New England Local Color Literature: A Women's Tradition* (New York: Ungar, 1988), considers Stowe a local-color writer; Gillian Brown (*Domestic Individualism: Imagining Self in Nineteenth Century America* (Berkeley and Los Angeles: Univ. of California Press, 1990) groups her with Hawthorne and Melville. See also Joan D. Hedrick, "Parlor Literature: Harriet Beecher Stowe and the Question of 'Great Women Artists,'" *Signs* 17, no. 2 (1992): 275–303.

30. Mary Kelley, *Private Woman, Public Stage: Literary Domesticity in Nineteenth-Century America* (New York: Oxford Univ. Press, 1984).

31. See Judith A. Roman, *Annie Adams Fields: The Spirit of Charles Street* (Bloomington: Indiana Univ. Press, 1990).

32. Rita K. Gollin, "Subordinated Power: Mrs. and Mr. James T. Fields," in Shirley Marchalonis, ed., *Patrons and Protégées: Gender, Friendship, and Writing in Nineteenth-Century America* (New Brunswick, N.J.: Rutgers Univ. Press, 1988), p. 157.

33. Donovan, *New England Local Color Literature* and *Sarah Orne Jewett* (New York: Ungar, 1980).

34. J. Roman, *Annie Adams Fields,* 26.

35. For examples see Fields, ed., *Letters:* "I have been reading an old copy of Donne's poems with perfect delight. They seem new to me just now, even the things I knew best. We must read many of them together" (p. 60); "I have been reading a really wonderful little book by poor Richard Jefferies. . . . [H]is ability to put into words the consciousness of life and individuality and relationship to eternity is something amazing. I have never known anything just like it. I thought of 'thy friend' [Whittier] as I read it" (pp. 71–2).

    Since writing this, my sense of the dense connections of reading, friendship, and selfhood has been confirmed and enriched by two essays: Helen Lefkowitz Horowitz's "'Nous Autres': Reading, Passion, and the Creation of M. Carey Thomas," *Journal of American History* 79 (1992): 68–95; and Marjorie Pryse's "Archives of Female Friendship and the 'Way' Jewett Wrote" (*New England Quarterly* 66 (1993): 47–66. I thank Martha Vicinus and Michael Bell, respectively, for calling them to my attention.

36. My understanding of heterosociality in late-nineteenth-century bourgeois culture is informed by an unpublished manuscript by David Scobey, "Sexual Order and Public Space in Victorian New York: The Ambiguities of Ladies' Mile," and also by his "Anatomy of the Prom-

enade: The Politics of Bourgeois Sociability in Nineteenth-Century New York," *Social History* 17 (1992): 203–27.

37. Quoted in Donovan, *New England Local Color Literature*, p. 1.

38. Since I wrote this essay, Richard Brodhead's *Cultures of Letters: Scenes of Reading and Writing in Nineteenth-Century America* (Chicago: Univ. of Chicago Press, 1993) has appeared, offering important arguments about the significance of the range of articles that appeared in the "quality" magazines and the cultural work done by local-color fiction in this period; he greatly extends some of the suggestions that follow. Brodhead's chapter on Jewett, like this volume of essays, seeks to historicize her work in terms of class and nation.

39. Eric Sundquist, "Realism and Regionalism," in Emory Elliott, ed., *Columbia Literary History of the United States* (New York: Columbia Univ. Press, 1988), 509.

40. I should perhaps reiterate that what I am observing is not a determinism, but the gendering of the system of generic classifications. Thus not all writers who are white women or persons of color write local-color fiction, and some white men do write local-color fiction; but a variety of mechanisms – internal to the writer, in the functioning of the market, and in the expectations of readers – push toward a coincidence of the identity of the writer and the writer's position in the system. The functioning of the system is also visible in the fact that, as Michael Bell notes in Chapter 3 of this volume, Jewett's Maine fiction receives far more critical attention than her other work.

41. Raymond Williams, *Writing in Society* (London: Verso, n.d.), 229–30. The essay was originally published in 1982.

42. Perry D. Westbrook, *Acres of Flint: Writers of Rural New England, 1870–1900* (Washington, D.C.: Scarecrow Press, 1951), pp. 11–12, 71.

43. James Cox, "Regionalism: A Diminished Thing," in Elliott, ed., *Columbia Literary History*, p. 767.

44. Sarah Orne Jewett, *The Country of the Pointed Firs and Other Stories*, ed. Mary Ellen Chase, intro. Marjorie Pryse (1896; rpt. New York: Norton, 1982), p. 28. All citations in the text are to this edition.

45. Sarah Orne Jewett, "Looking Back on Girlhood" (1892), rpt. in *The Uncollected Short Stories of Sarah Orne Jewett*, ed. and intro. Richard Cary (Waterville, Me.: Colby College Press, 1971), p. 6.

46. "I am getting quite ambitious and really feel that writing is my work – my business perhaps; and it is so much better than making an amusement of it as I used. . . . I am glad to have something to do in the world and something which may prove very helpful and useful if I care to make it so, which I certainly do." Jewett to Scudder, 1873, in

Richard Cary, ed., *Sarah Orne Jewett Letters* (Waterville, Me.: Colby College Press, 1956), p. 27.

47. See Ammons, "Jewett's Witches," as well as the biographical sources on Jewett.

48. On this topic I recommend particularly the essays by Richard Cary ("The Literary Rubrics of Sarah Orne Jewett") and Josephine Donovan ("Sarah Orne Jewett's Critical Theory: Notes toward a Feminine Literary Mode") in Nagel, ed., *Critical Essays;* see also chap. 6 of Donovan's *Sarah Orne Jewett.* On imagination, see the letter to Aldrich in Fields, ed., *Letters,* pp. 78–80. Jewett quotes the familiar Arnold tag about "the best" in a letter to Cather; ibid., p. 248.

49. The Howells comment is quoted in Bell's essay in this volume (Chapter 3, n. 12); the Kipling as part of Fields's introduction to *Letters,* p. 9. It is only fair to add that Fields tells us this letter gave Jewett "unending pleasure."

50. Van Wyck Brooks, *New England: Indian Summer, 1865–1915* (New York: Dutton, 1940), p. 353. See Frost, *Sarah Orne Jewett,* pp. 105–6, for an assessment of the biographical evidence on this point.

51. Everett Carter, *Howells and the Age of Realism* (New York: Lippincott, 1954), p. 120.

52. Laurel Thatcher Ulrich, *A Midwife's Tale: The Life of Martha Ballard, Based on Her Diary, 1785–1812* (New York: Random House, 1990).

53. For a broad context see Gerald Graff, *Professing Literature: An Institutional History* (Chicago: Univ. of Chicago Press, 1987).

54. See (in addition to Graff) Paul Lauter, "Race and Gender in the Shaping of the American Literary Canon: A Case Study from the Twenties," *Feminist Studies* 9 (1983): 435–63; Nina Baym, "Melodramas of Beset Manhood: How Theories of American Fiction Exclude Women Authors," *American Quarterly* 33 (1981): 123–39; and Sharon O'Brien, "Becoming Noncanonical: The Case Against Willa Cather," in Cathy N. Davidson, ed., *Reading in America: Literature and Social History* (Baltimore: Johns Hopkins Univ. Press, 1989).

55. Richard Poirier, *A World Elsewhere: The Place of Style in American Literature* (New York: Oxford Univ. Press, 1966).

56. O'Brien, "Becoming Noncanonical," pp. 240–58; the quotations are from pp. 250–1. Granville Hicks is the immediate source of the hostile characterization of Jewett.

57. No one seems to have observed that placing "The Queen's Twin" earlier and "William's Wedding" at the end of the novel would have created a far more plausible sequence.

58. Elizabeth Ammons, *Conflicting Stories: American Women Writers at the*

Turn into the Twentieth Century (New York: Oxford Univ. Press, 1991), 52.

59. Sandra A. Zagarell, "Narrative of Community: The Identification of a Genre," *Signs* 13 (1988): 498–527.

60. Marcia McClintock Folsom, "'Tact Is a Kind of Mind-Reading': Empathic Style in Sarah Orne Jewett's *The Country of the Pointed Firs*," *Colby Library Quarterly,* 18 (1982): 66–78. Reprinted in Nagel, ed., *Critical Essays,* 76–89. The quotations from Folsom are from p. 77; the quotation from Jewett appears on p. 46 of the Chase edition.

61. S. Sherman, *Sarah Orne Jewett, an American Persephone.*

62. Donovan uses this phrase in the title of her chapter on Jewett in *New England Local Color Literature.*

63. M. Roman, *Sarah Orne Jewett: Reconstructing Gender,* p. ix.

64. Denise Riley, *"Am I That Name?" Feminism and the Category of 'Women' in History* (Minneapolis: Univ. of Minnesota Press, 1988); see also Nancy F. Cott's "Feminist Theory and Feminist Movements: The Past Before Us," in Juliet Mitchell and Ann Oakley, eds., *What is Feminism? A Re-examination* (New York: Pantheon, 1986), pp. 49–62, as well as her *Grounding of Modern Feminism* (New Haven, Conn.: Yale Univ. Press, 1987).

65. See Eric Hobsbawm and Terence Ranger, eds., *The Invention of Tradition* (New York: Cambridge Univ. Press, 1983).

66. Amy Kaplan, "Nation, Region, and Empire," in Emory Elliott, ed., *Columbia History of the American Novel* (New York: Columbia Univ. Press, 1991), pp. 250–1.

67. Judith Fetterley and Marjorie Pryse, Preface, *American Women Regionalists, 1850–1910: A Norton Anthology* (New York: Norton, 1992), xvii.

68. Cary, ed., *Letters,* 19–20.

69. Jay Martin, *Harvests of Change: American Literature, 1865–1914* (Englewood Cliffs, N.J.: Prentice-Hall, 1967), p. 143; Marilyn Sanders Mobley, *Folk Roots and Mythic Wings in Sarah Orne Jewett and Toni Morrison* (Baton Rouge: Louisiana State Univ. Press, 1991).

70. Fetterley and Pryse, Preface to *American Women Regionalists.* p. xvii.

71. To cite just one example in each category: on journalism, see "Fame's Little Day"; on layoffs, "The Gray Mills of Farley"; on tourism as an industry, "An Every-Day Girl"; on immigrants, "Little French Mary."

72. Anthony Giddens, *The Consequences of Modernity* (Stanford, Calif.: Stanford Univ. Press, 1990), p. 64.

73. Sarah Orne Jewett, *Old Friends and New* (Boston: Houghton, Osgood, 1879), pp. 82, 95.

74. See Giddens, *Consequences of Modernity,* pp. 18–19.

75. See Glenda Hobbs, "Pure and Passionate: Female Friendship in Sarah Orne Jewett's 'Martha's Lady,'" in Nagel, ed., *Critical Essays*, pp. 99–107.

76. Kasson, *Rudeness and Civility.*

77. Louis A. Renza, *"A White Heron" and the Question of Minor Literature* (Madison: Univ. of Wisconsin Press, 1984).

78. Charles Taylor, *Sources of the Self: The Making of the Modern Identity* (Cambridge, Mass.: Harvard Univ. Press, 1989). The first phrase is the title of Part III; the quotation is from p. 224.

79. For the frame of reference of this comment, see Benedict Anderson, *Imagined Communities: Reflections on the Origin and Spread of Nationalism* (London: Verso, 1983). See also Amy Kaplan, "Romancing the Empire: The Embodiment of American Masculinity in the Popular Historical Novel of the 1890s," *American Literary History* 2 (1990): 659–90.

80. Walter Benjamin, *Illuminations*, trans. Harry Zohn, ed. and intro. Hannah Arendt (New York: Schocken, 1969), p. 256.

81. Cather, *Not Under Forty*, p. 81. Each of these comments, of course, bears the marks of its own historicity — visible in Benjamin's teleological notion of stages of civilization and Cather's allegiance to an ideology of individual achievement.

2

Country's Portrayal of Community and the Exclusion of Difference

SANDRA A. ZAGARELL

A LOOK of delight came into the faces of those who recognized the plain, dear old figure [of Mrs. Blacket] beside me; one revelation after another was made of the constant interest and intercourse that had linked [Green Island] and [the] scattered farms into a golden chain of love and dependence," Jewett's narrator remarks early in the Bowden reunion section of *The Country of the Pointed Firs*.[1] In a very different vein, another guest comments later, "Somebody observed once that you could pick out the likeness of most every sort of a foreigner when you looked about you in our parish . . . I always did think Mari' Harris resembled a Chinee" (p. 101).

Reading the first passage, one may savor the empathic understanding of community that has made Jewett's *Country* so moving for many readers, myself included.[2] Reading the second, with its use of the racist slur "Chinee" to dismiss a woman unpopular among Dunnet Landing folk and excluded from the community celebrated in Jewett's famous narrative, probably makes other readers as uncomfortable as it makes me. Most commentators seem to have responded simply by ignoring it. Except for a single essay written in 1957, Ferman Bishop's "Sarah Orne Jewett's Ideas of Race," there is virtually no critical discussion of Jewett's views on race and little serious consideration of the genteel elitism evident in much of her writing. What little acknowledgment there is takes the form of an aside. Warner Berthoff's landmark 1959 article, "The Art of Jewett's *Pointed Firs*," notes circumspectly that "readers of her letters and other work know that she was not free of certain 'hysterias' of her time and society" and cites Bishop's essay in a footnote; Josephine Donovan mentions her racial attitudes in connection with a few short stories, calling the "blatantly racist" "A War Debt" (1895) "one of Jewett's few but unfortunate lapses"; Sarah Sherman indicates that she was a Tory.[3]

The central concern of *Country* is the construction of community. And it seems to me impossible to understand what "community" in the book is without exploring the racial attitudes, nativism, and exclusionary impulses that inflect the narrative's graceful, appealing depiction of community. To fail to engage in such an exploration is to lift "community" in *Country* out of its context and to generalize codes, cues, and references that are historically specific. Similarly, to assume that *Country's* community extends to everyone is to generalize what is actually the portrayal of a single group – longtime Maine residents, especially those of French descent, and readers like them – thereby obscuring the text's exclusions and omissions. In historicizing the community of *Country*, however, I wish to avoid judging it by present-day standards or hectoring it into accountability to ideas about the representation of race or ethnicity current in the late twentieth century. Rather, I wish to place Jewett's narrative within her era, particularly her own cultural and class milieu. Such an enterprise makes it clear that what have been celebrated as universal, reader-embracing qualities, such as *Country's* weblike structure and Dunnet Landing's matrifocality, are really both inclusive *and* restrictive. They contribute to a dynamic representation of community that continually traces the bonds among community participants, but at the same time they tacitly create a racially specific community and contribute to the figurative exclusion of those significantly different from community members.

I

Many of the New England Brahmins who formed Jewett's circle of friends in and around Boston felt America was under siege during the 1880s and 1890s, when Jewett did most of her major work. Immigration to the United States increased radically, the steady stream of Irish immigrants joined by waves of newcomers from southern Europe and the Slavic countries.[4] Cities continued their rapid growth and slums began to be a matter of a widespread concern; industrialization intensified and violent labor conflicts, of which the Pullman and Homestead strikes are the best known, escalated. These were decades during which the prominence of New England's elite was on the wane: when one-third of the population of Boston was foreign, the Irish were beginning to dominate Boston politics, and New England was no longer the main source of the nation's political or cultural leaders.

During this period, not surprisingly, many members of Jewett's class were deeply nativist. They believed that "America" had been, and should remain, a homogeneous nation – a nation whose origins were usually identified as Anglo-Saxon. For example, Jewett's close friend Thomas Bailey Aldrich – editor of the *Atlantic Monthly* from 1881 to 1890, when Jewett published much of her work in that magazine – was vehemently opposed to the unchecked influx of foreigners. Along with Henry Cabot Lodge, he was one of the most prominent proponents of the Immigration Restriction League (founded in Boston in 1894), which, according to literary historian Jay Martin, lamented "the loss of homogeneity and promulgate[ed] a myth of Anglo-Saxon superiority."[5] Aldrich's poem "Unguarded Gates" (published in the *Atlantic Monthly* in July 1892) articulates much of the League's sentiment. Its second stanza begins, "Wide open and unguarded stand our gates / And through them presses a wild motley throng" and asks "O Liberty, white Goddess! Is it well / To leave the gates unguarded?" After the speaker's horrified evocation of various ethnic groups, the poem cautions that an unchecked tide of immigrants could destroy American liberty much as the Goths and Vandals trampled Rome.[6]

In the 1890s, the Malayans, Scythians, Slavs, and others Aldrich named were considered races. "Race" had no precise meaning during this period; it could refer to what we currently call language groups, to ethnic groups, to cultures, or to nations. Climate, natural environment, and physical characteristics were considered important factors in the creation of a "race"; a discrete language and culture were seen as its preeminent properties. "Race" was a key explanatory category in late-nineteenth-century thought. Theories about racial differences and the relative evolution and superiority of northern, Nordic, or Teutonic races, Romantic in origin and buttressed by Darwinian biology and social Darwinism, dominated much German and English and some French thinking. In the United States, too, by the time of the Spanish-American War, as historian Thomas Gossett puts it, "the idea of race superiority had deeply penetrated nearly every field – biology, sociology, history, literature, and political science." According to this thinking, Anglo-Saxons were the superior race.[7]

By the mid-1880s, hierarchical racialized thinking was also central to Jewett's mentality. She was partly of French descent, and like that of a number of Brahmins – including Lodge and Henry Adams – her version of Nordicism cherished the "Northmen" who had become the Normans of France. She felt that the best of America was Anglo-Norman. Her book for children, *The Story of the Normans* (Putnam's Story of the Nations series, 1886), takes for granted a hierarchy of races based on traits presumed innate. Attributing courage, energy, taste, and gentility to the Normans, she assumes that they remained a discrete race from the time of their Norse origins through their settlement in medieval Normandy, the Norman invasion of England in 1066, and English settlement of the United States, retaining their purity even in late-nineteenth-century America. Contemplating England's greatness, for instance, she links the traits she celebrates in the Normans with England's expansionist world leadership: whether "the Norman spirit leads [England] to be self-confident or headstrong and willful, or the Saxon spirit holds her back into slowness and dullness, and lack of proper perception in emergencies or epochs of necessary change, still she follows the right direction and leads the way."[8] Jewett concludes her history by envisioning a family-like alliance of modern nations united by Norman blood: "To-day the Northman, the Norman, and the Englishman, and a young nation on this western shore of the Atlantic are all kindred who, possessing a rich inheritance, should own the closest of kindred ties" (*SON*, p. 66).[9]

Racialized thinking and an assumption that "racial" homogeneity was desirable thus formed one context for the portrayal of community in *Country*. Dunnet inhabitants, the unnamed narrator, and the text's readers are all assumed to share a specifically American culture whose origins are northern European.[10] The association of a village community with the "true" America is, moreover,

characteristic of the literary tradition to which *Country* most cen-
trally belongs, for Jewett's loving evocation of Dunnet Landing is a
narrative of community. The representation of community is a
central thematic and structural concern of this strain of prose narrative, which began to appear in the United States early in the
nineteenth century.[11] Communities take different forms in narratives of community, reflecting the fact that in the nineteenth century "community" was a contested concept, as it is in the twentieth.
In the antebellum period, for example, most narratives of community envisioned "America" as a homogeneous community, usually
a New England village united by a fixed social structure and a
single religion, often Congregationalism. Harriet Beecher Stowe's
pre–*Uncle Tom* village sketches are typical of this literature. A few,
however, including Lydia Huntley Sigourney's *Sketch of Connecticut,
Forty Years Since* (1824), presented the most genuinely "American"
community as one that accommodated diverse religious and racial
groups.[12]

Given Jewett's beliefs and temperament, and her history of having lived much of her life in the coastal Maine village of South
Berwick, it is understandable that *Country* features a long-lived,
stable, and homogeneous community. One of her stated sources of
literary inspiration, Stowe's *The Pearl of Orr's Island* (1862), may
well have contributed as well to her equation of community with
uniformity, continuity, and quintessential Americanness, for Stowe
venerated the history, culture, and social traditions she associated
with New England. Both writers, like many other nineteenth-
century authors of narratives of community, moreover, saw New
England as the repository of what was most valuable in America as
a nation.

II

While many readers have recognized that *Country*'s structure and
its vision cannot be separated, the work of Elizabeth Ammons and
Joseph Allen Boone has been particularly significant in establishing the connection between *Country*'s narrative structure and its
representation of community.[13] Ammons and Boone show that
Country eschews the kind of individual-based, linear, developmen-

43

tal plot characteristic of most nineteenth-century novels in favor of a weblike structure that expands in a radial or circular manner from the community's center, the home of Almira Todd.[14] *Country's* circular design, I suggest in this essay, is complemented by a narrative technique of intensification through repetition – that is, a persistent emphasis on and reiteration of key structural and thematic aspects of the narrative. Repetition makes the community at Dunnet seem both dynamic and fixed, unchanging. It also inscribes the community's exemption from the turbulence and change prominent in the United States at large. In focusing on the ways in which repetition gives the portrayal of community depth and vitality, the following discussion therefore necessarily also explores how *Country* actively *produces* Dunnet as a pure and homogeneous community.

Consider, first, the representation of natural environment. *Country* erases all the markers of industrialism and other conditions of late-nineteenth-century life that existed in Jewett's own village. South Berwick was a stop on the railroad. The remnants of a considerable shipyard blighted the village wharf, and textile mills flourished a mile away; the local population included Irish immigrant laborers.[15] Dunnet's setting, by contrast, is purely pastoral; moreover, as Jewett's title asserts, this setting helps characterize the community. Repeatedly referring to Maine's firs and spruces, *Country* posits these trees as autochthonous, indigenous; they stand for the Dunnet community as a whole, giving it an air of being native and natural to its particular environment. Mrs. Todd repeats and extends this asserted equivalency between the natural environment and the community through her frequent analogies between plants and people. This naturalization is also repeated by large-scale narrative design, *Country's* radial or centric structure. Patterned on the movement of the narrator, and sometimes Mrs. Todd, back and forth from the latter's home to the community's margins and outer limits (the schoolhouse, Green Island, Shell-heap Island, the Bowden farm, Elijah Tilley's fish house and home), this structure narrativizes place by reiterating its contours. Like the autocthonous tree, it makes the Dunnet community seem entirely local, congruent with its particular geography and none other.

In casting Dunnet as local and organic, this multileveled naturalizing also conveys the community's separateness from the urban society from which the narrator hails. The organization of the Dunnet community itself similarly asserts this separateness, accentuating Dunnet's harmony. As many feminist critics have noted, Dunnet is matrifocal. The relationship between Mrs. Todd and Mrs. Blacket, established by the trip to Green Island, constitutes the emotional center of the community as well as its ideal relationship. The narrative repeats and elaborates this tie's matrifocality. As Elizabeth Ammons has shown, in the climactic scene in which Mrs. Todd and the narrator gather the medicinal herb pennyroyal, Mrs. Todd becomes mother-like and the narrator her daughter. By the Bowden reunion chapters, the entire community seems formed around its mothers. Almost everyone who figures in *Country* seems to be a Bowden, and the gathering is resonant with evocations of motherhood, with the oldest mother present, Mrs. Blackett, the celebration's acknowledged "queen."

While this matrifocality nominally repudiates the patriarchal family that predominated in late-nineteenth-century America by making mothers seem in charge, in privileging the traditional family as an institution it also defines the community within the parameters of a conservative structure. That is, it limits the roles possible within the community to familial ones – in *Country*, these extend beyond mother and daughter to son, brother, sister, cousin, with fathers being conspicuously absent. Friendships are sister-like; Mrs. Todd and Mrs. Fosdick, who were girls together, talk frequently about their mothers, siblings, and other relatives. Mapping "community" onto "family" is another way of naturalizing the community: family roles would have seemed organic to nineteenth-century readers. In effect, in being created on the basis of real or fictive kinship, the community perpetuates its homogeneity. It cannot, by definition, admit anyone alien without contravening its identity. By implication, those who do not belong probably should not. While Jewett's accent is on inclusion, with the community extending beyond the Bowdens to embrace the narrator, this inclusion actually confirms Dunnet's homogeneity, since the narrator is like the Bowdens in important cultural ways and she adapts to the family model in becoming like a daughter to Mrs. Todd.

As it extends the community/family identification, *Country* accentuates the restrictiveness of the community by calling attention to the Bowdens' racial particularity.[16] The Bowden reunion section establishes the family's French and Anglo-Norman descent. Mrs. Todd confirms the narrator's guess that the family is French in origin, and the latter reflects that the "early settlers on this northern coast of New England were of Huguenot blood, and . . . it is the Norman Englishman, not the Saxon, who goes adventuring to a new world" (p. 102). The racial theories that ranked the Normans at the top of a comprehensive racial hierarchy in *The Story of the Normans* also inform the narrator's observations of the Bowdens. She identifies them as superior to "most country people," citing a gentility that seems, to use a modern term, genetic: an "inheritance of good taste and skill and a pleasing gift of formality" (p. 105). These equations between Normans and Bowdens and among family, community, and race add another dimension to the naturalizing of the Dunnet community, rendering its homogeneity and worth a matter of long-established heredity.

These associations are amplified, moreover, to include the United States as a nation. At the end of the Bowden celebrations, the reunion is compared to "the great national anniversaries which our country has lately kept" (the centennial, the thirtieth anniversary of the Civil War). Observing that "blood is thicker than water," even when it is somewhat "adulterated," the narrator conflates family and nation in a generalization that embraces all bona fide members (or citizens) but clearly excludes those from different racial/national families. "Clannishness is an instinct of the heart," she reflects; "it is more than a birthright or a custom; and lesser rights were forgotten in the claim to a common inheritance" (p. 110). America itself, in this formulation, is a "clan," both familial and racial. Citizenship, by implication, is natural and inborn; it is endowed by an organic quality, "instinct," not by "birthright or custom." As the analogies and equations multiply, the Dunnet family becomes the essence of the American nation, and what is truly American seems to be Anglo-Norman. The community of Dunnet comes to exemplify the tenet Jewett had articulated in *The Story of the Normans*, that "the people of the United States . . . might be called the Normans of modern times" (*SON*, p. 360).

46

Seen in this context, the construction of difference, a matter of considerable concern in *Country,* also discloses racial overtones. One form of difference, individual idiosyncrasy, is figured as indigenous — variation within the group or, to use a favorite Jewett term, "stock" to which community members belong. The Dunnet eccentrics — William Blackett, Captain Littlepage, Joanna Todd — are associated with local flora, aligned thereby with the community and its natural environment; they are, for example, "strayaway folks" who are like "strayaway plants" (p. 102). But the text refuses such a classification to the resident of Dunnet Landing who does not conform to community mores and is rude and abrasive, Mari' Harris. To her is applied the racial epithet to which I referred at the beginning of this essay, "Chinee." Invoked as it is at the Bowden reunion, this appellation asserts absolute difference not only between Mari' and the community but also between her and the nation for which the community is a model. Indeed, it identifies her with the single race that was formally debarred from the United States by acts of Congress: the Chinese Exclusion Acts of 1882, 1888, and 1891. Read alongside the connections *Country* makes among family, community, and nation, the epithet "Chinee" also points to the ideal of a United States preserved from continuing racial diversification. Jewett would never have employed the kind of crude, derogatory racial categories on which Senator James Blaine relied when he spoke in Congress in 1879 in support of excluding the Chinese — "Either the Anglo-Saxon race will possess the Pacific slope . . . or the Mongolians will possess it." "[Asians cannot] make a homogeneous element [with Americans]."[17] Nevertheless, in the climactic Bowden reunion scene, in which the Dunnet community is given its most formal articulation, *Country* does echo the more genteel advocacy of racial exclusion articulated by members of Jewett's Boston circle like Thomas Bailey Aldrich.

Many of *Country's* other formal and stylistic features affirm the Dunnet community as homogeneous and tightly boundaried. The narrative features the microdynamics of community life, proceeding according to a rhythm I have elsewhere called "perpetual negotiation."[18] Brilliantly establishing as the pulse of each scene community members' verbal give-and-take and their exchanges of food, succor, and information, these negotiations constitute an extraordinary accomplishment, bringing everyday community activities to life and representing the community as stable, yet always in process. Among American writers before Jewett, perhaps only Stowe in *The Pearl of Orr's Island* and *The Minister's Wooing* equals this achievement. These negotiations also, however, assert the community's autonomy, its separateness from the national economy, for they depict the community producing or procuring locally all the meager resources it requires: foods like fish, potatoes, onions, lobsters; Mrs. Todd's herbal medicines; the shirts Mrs. Blackett sews, the socks Elijah Tilley knits. The many conversations and instances of storytelling likewise convey the self-sustaining character of the community's culture. While stories like those told by Captain Littlepage and Elijah Tilley can be monotonous, community members' reiteration of their own histories or those of people they have known keep community traditions alive. Mrs. Todd and Mrs. Fosdick's retelling of the story of Joanna Todd, who secluded herself on a remote island in penitence for the bitterness she felt after being jilted, demonstrates vividly the way storytelling preserves and perpetuates community self-definition. A joint endeavor through which two old friends achieve "happy harmony" where they had earlier disagreed (p. 69), this retelling affirms the community norms that Joanna had so vigorously repudiated, figuratively reclaiming for the community a woman who had literally resisted such integration. As the friends retell Joanna's story, they collaborate in explaining her withdrawal in familiar Dunnet Landing terms. Always "poor Joanna," she "was full o' feeling, and her troubles hurt her more than she could bear" (p. 69); her mentality was natural, "like bad eyesight," for which there is no "remedy" (pp. 77–8). The retelling of stories, as this incident shows, reinscribes numerous community boundaries: it provides a way to embrace recalcitrant or resistant members; it reweaves community bonds; it preserves and transmits the community's culture. In maintaining these boundaries, storytelling, like other elements of the narrative, implicitly draws a circle around the community, in effect keeping out the kind of person who cannot understand its language and the kind about whom no story is told.

III

Despite its affirmations of Dunnet's autonomy, *Country* continually locates the town within the circumstances of contemporary American life that it seems to have banished. Dunnet's character, though repeatedly evoked as natural, is shown to have resulted partly from historical forces. Its matrifocality resulted from the Civil War deaths or western migration of many of the men; its "purity" was made possible by the decline of the whaling and shipping industries. The most dramatic expression of the connection between the community and the nation, however, is conceptual, not historical: namely, the perpetual linkage embedded in the narrator, who acts as both participant and observer. This narrator's very position straddles a dichotomy that lay at the heart of nineteenth-century social thinking: the distinction between *Gemeinschaft* and *Gesellschaft*.[19] These concepts, which translate, roughly, as "community" and "society," were thought to describe separate and contrasting forms of group life. *Gemeinschaft* refers to the organic or "natural" community life thought to precede industrialism and capitalism. Imbued with formal rituals, having a strong sacred dimension, *Gemeinschaft* was conceived as grounded in the family, its members identifying, not individually, but as members of the group. In *Gesellschaft*, of which late-nineteenth-century urban American life was one instance, the individual is the fundamental unit and group associations are contractual, entered into by individuals on the basis of self-interest. The narrator's experiences of life in Dunnet Landing and her representation of it cast the Dunnet community as a *Gemeinschaft*.[20] The joy with which she gives herself over to Dunnet life attests to its *Gemeinschaft*-like authenticity and simplicity, and its uniformity makes coming to know it seem epistemologically and emotionally undemanding, the equivalent, as she says, of "becoming acquainted with a single person" (pp. 1–2). The way she appears to transcribe community life, in its entirety, into the narrative, understanding and reproducing community language effortlessly, further attests to a simplicity that seems appealing and accessible.

While appearing to present Dunnet Landing on its own terms, however, the narrator repeatedly locates it in relation to contemporary urban America. Constantly subjecting her experiences to explanation and interpretation, she grounds virtually all her reflections in cosmopolitan epistemological categories that posit "community" not only as different from "society" but as "better," more authentic, more whole. Frequently, for example, she uses phrases and concepts that establish the connection between Dunnet and urban America as a contrast between genuineness and artificiality. "Simple" and its variants are among her favorite terms for Dunnet ways and people – yet "simplicity" and its frequent companion, "innocence," acquire meaning only in relation to their opposites. Things are simple in comparison with the complex, innocent in comparison with the worldly. Similarly, when she says of Mrs. Blackett, "She was a delightful little person herself with bright eyes and an affectionate air of expectation like a child on holiday" (p. 36), the analogy and the words "delightful" and "little" are patronizing, casting Mrs. Blackett as someone unjaded by the difficult conditions with which the narrator and her readers are familiar. Even the narrator's most compassionate statements about Mrs. Todd tacitly posit her mentor as a sort of noble primitive to be appreciated by sophisticated readers. Recounting her exchange with Mrs. Todd in the climactic scene in which they gather pennyroyal on Green Island, she observes that "an absolute, archaic grief possessed this countrywoman." Used in conjunction with "countrywoman," "archaic" makes the rural way of life of which Mrs. Todd is representative seem whole but also obsolete, the remnant of a bygone era in which emotions were starker and ran deeper than in urban America.

Country's representation of its readership not only further inscribes this dichotomy; it explicitly positions the narrative as an evocation of *Gemeinschaft* intended to benefit not Dunnet members, but urbanites such as readers of the *Atlantic Monthly,* who would perceive Dunnet as an expression of their own origins and a repository of what was best and most genuine in themselves.[21] Framing the community by the narrator's visit of a summer and frequently evoking readers as "you" and "we," a class of people located outside of Dunnet and much like the narrator, *Country* locates the importance of this Maine community in the boost its example offers to such readers. In the post-*Country* Dunnet tale

"William's Wedding," the narrator refers to these readers explicitly, obliquely articulating as the narrative's objectives their vicarious escape from contemporary life and consequent replenishment. Her narrative, she says there, is "written for those who have a Dunnet Landing of their own: who either kindly share this with the writer, or possess another" (p. 217). Dunnet Landing is fictitious. The narrative cannot, therefore, be intended for actual residents of Dunnet. We can assume that what is important is what the representation of Dunnet gives outside readers. This is also suggested in the passage's evocation of designated readers' proprietary attitudes; in "having," "sharing," or "possessing" a Dunnet Landing, they may experience the kind of personal restoration often sought by tourists visiting the country.

Bridging the gap between *Gemeinschaft* and *Gesellschaft*, *Country's* narrator models the affirmation for her designated readers this representation of community provides. She tacks back and forth between the position of a participant in the community and that of an observer who can identify with Dunnet life. First she describes Dunnet life as she experiences it or as members convey it to her through stories; then she makes interpretive statements that articulate the significance Dunnet's life has for her and her readers, who apparently resemble her. Typically she renders a scene or recounts an experience by incorporating Dunnet members' language, then reflecting on it in a discourse that encompasses such subjects as classical culture, racial theory, and the history of Western civilization and generalizes about psychology, aesthetics, and group life. This discourse emerges from the culture of her designated readers, not from the culture of Dunnet Landing. It casts the Dunnet community as the source and sanctuary of qualities she, and they, hold supreme. After hearing the story of Joanna Todd, for instance, she makes a pilgrimage to Shell-heap Island, where Joanna lived in self-imposed exile. As she stands at Joanna's grave, she explains what Joanna's story "means" in terms far more comprehensive than the emotional, biological, and religious formulations of Mrs. Todd and Mrs. Fosdick. Joanna's grave, she muses, will always have visitors, because "the world cannot forget [such people], try as it may; the feet of the young find them out because of curiosity and dim foreboding, while the old bring hearts full of remembrance" (p. 82). Speaking of "the world," "the young," "the old," referring to the "remembrance" common to the last and the "dim foreboding" of the second, she identifies Joanna as one instance of a profound truth about human isolation.

Even when she negotiates between experience and interpretation in a more integrated fashion, the narrator expresses the significance of Dunnet life in a manner that renders Dunnet exemplary. Thus, recounting the visit to Green Island, she moves between voicing her immediate impression of Mrs. Blackett and articulating the insights about human relations these responses suggest to her:

> Her hospitality was something exquisite; she had the gift which so many women lack, of being able to make themselves and their houses belong entirely to a guest's pleasure. . . . Tact is after all a kind of mindreading. . . . Sometimes, as I watched her eager, sweet old face, I wondered why she had been set to shine on this lonely island of the northern coast. It must have been to keep the balance true, and make up to all her scattered and depending neighbors for other things which they may have lacked. (pp. 46–7)

Like the generalizations just discussed, these statements about communal qualities such as hospitality, tact, and balance seem axiomatic. They seem intended to uplift readers who, though living in fragmented urban circumstances, can, like the narrator, appreciate and identify with the principles the community members personify with such purity.

Balance and the other distinctive features of Dunnet life may seem universal and all-inclusive as well as axiomatic. Yet they are expressed in a general context that complements the assertion of Dunnet's Anglo-Norman heritage and *Country's* cultural and racial restrictiveness. The narrator characterizes members of the community as inheritors of classical Greek traditions, in effect also characterizing readers who can understand the classical references she makes as inheritors of this tradition. Dunnet inhabitants live out such traditions instinctively; readers are more sophisticated and may be self-conscious about their heritage. Classical references proliferate in the chapters on the Bowden reunion, where they explicitly position the Dunnet community as a nineteenth-century descendant of Greek civilization. Of the Bowdens' procession the narrator muses, "We might have been a company of ancient

Greeks going to celebrate a victory, or to worship the god of harvests, in the grove above." She does generalize to all family celebrations — "The sky, the sea, have watched poor humanity at its rites so long; we were no more a New England family celebrating its own existence and simple progress" — but the next sentence reconfigures the connection between the Bowdens and classical Greece, conceived in Jewett's day as the childhood of the best of Western civilization: "We possessed the instincts of a far, forgotten childhood: I found myself thinking that we ought to be carrying green branches and singing as we went" (p. 100).

These references are instances of Hellenism, the celebration of the cultural superiority of Greece that flourished in Europe and the United States in the nineteenth century and that, as Martin Bernal has shown, had strong racial overtones. In its popularization in Victorian England, Hellenism not only articulated valued cultural traits but relied on racial argument in claiming a classical origin for England. The "ultimate appeal" by which Matthew Arnold's famous *Culture and Anarchy*, probably Victorian England's most influential Hellenist work, asserts England as a nation with Hellenic rather than Hebraic roots was, as Bernal puts it, "to race." Arnold maintained that "Hellenism is an Indo-European growth. Hebrewism is a Semitic growth. England is an Indo-European nation. Thus it would seem to belong naturally to the movement of Hellenism."[22]

The line connecting Jewett to Arnold is direct. She met him when he stayed at the home of Annie Fields during his 1883–4 visit to the United States, she and Annie Fields visited Arnold's widow and children when they were in England in 1892, she knew and honored Arnold's work, and she quotes him in her letters and her published fiction. For her, as for him, "Hellenism" was a marker of what is enduring and transcendent in culture. In an important letter that explains the way she saw much of her own literary practice, she links her work with Arnoldian Hellenism. Invoking a "department of literature" whose subject is "the good men and women of a village such as" South Berwick, she describes the literature she writes by adapting the famous phrase with which Arnold characterized the tragedies of Sophocles and articulated his criteria for "great" literature. The "department of literature" to which she refers, she indicates, is able to "see life steadily, and see it whole."²³

Locating characters much like "the good men and women" of South Berwick within Hellenic tradition, we have seen, is one way in which *Country's* narrator establishes the community's significance. Although the evocations of Greek culture and the assertion that Greek familial celebrations occurred during the "childhood" of the Bowden clan may seem to late-twentieth-century readers to universalize the Dunnet community, they actually restrict Dunnet to "races" thought to have descended from ancient Greece – northern Europeans, the British, the French. If nineteenth-century European Hellenism explicitly excluded African and Semitic "races," as Bernal shows (Asian "races" did not even come into question), Jewett's "American Hellenism" similarly, if implicitly, presented American culture as pure, worthy of preservation from the taint of alien ways. That is to say, what critics have often read as *Country's* apparent appeal to universality is an aspect of Nordicist discourse that quite specifically valorized "northern" races.²⁴

When *Country* initially appeared in the *Atlantic Monthly* in serial form in 1896, it concluded with the chapters on the Bowden reunion. Jewett added the final two chapters, "Along Shore" and "The Backward View," when it was published in book form later that year. For *Country's* first readers, then, the narrative's final vision resembled the one Jewett strove for at the end of *The Story of the Normans,* where she evokes a family of Norman descendants on both sides of the Atlantic. At least one nineteenth-century reader, the fine regionalist writer Alice Brown, registered the racial and cultural implications of *Country*. Reviewing the version we read today, she wrote, "The pointed firs have their roots in the ground of national being. The Reunion indeed bears a larger significance than its name. It stirs in us the dormant clan-spirit; we understand ancestor-worship, the continuity of being. . . . [Y]our mind marches grandly with the Bowdens, you throb like them with the pride of race, you acquiesce willingly in the sweet, loyal usages of domesticity."²⁵ Like Jewett, Brown elides nation, race, and family; her reference to her readers as "you" and "we" echoes Jewett's usage, suggesting how common and unremarkable was the assumption that American writers and readers were of one race and class.

By the time Willa Cather edited a version of *Country* in 1925, these elisions and assumptions had been transmuted into claims of universality – Cather singled out *Country*'s "message in a universal language" as the basis for a general appeal that later readers, too, have usually assumed for it.[26] Yet Jewett herself provides us with a point of entry for examining the limitations of Dunnet and the connections between *Country*'s moving representative of community and its exclusionary vision. In a later Dunnet story, provocatively entitled "The Foreigner" (1900), she problematizes the kind of homogeneity and nativism she celebrates in *Country*. Evoking the unhappy experience of life in Dunnet Landing for French, Catholic Mrs. Tolland, who lived most of her life in the Caribbean and whose first husband was Portuguese, she dramatizes Dunnet's repudiation of a foreigner whose class, sexual expressiveness, religion, culture, and nationality set her apart from the community. The later story makes no references to Dunnet members' racial and cultural heritage, and Dunnet folk, far from being gracious and hospitable, are depicted as hidebound, self-righteous, and cold – even Mrs. Todd is begrudging about "neighboring" with Mrs. Tolland, and only Mrs. Blackett welcomes her wholeheartedly. "The Foreigner" also casts some doubt on the racialized thinking of *Country*. It hints that Mrs. Tolland may be of mixed race – not only is she associated with the Caribbean, she is apparently darker than Dunnet residents. The possibility that she is a creole in no way diminishes the legitimacy of her claim to membership in the Dunnet community, and it implies that her ostracization (for which "The Foreigner" questions and exposes Dunnet Landing) may have a racial dimension. Read in conjunction with *Country*, then, "The Foreigner" seems to call into question the nationalism and Nordicism that, as we have seen, inform and help shape the earlier narrative.[27]

The path I have pursued in this essay – subjecting the racial and cultural exclusions of *Country*'s community to close historical and structural scrutiny – can be taken in many directions. One could, for instance, explore connections between the portrayal of com-

munity in *Country* (and in other late-nineteenth-century regionalist literature) as pastorally pure and the kind of tourism that currently features Maine as an attractive refuge for city dwellers, the
"Vacationland" advertised by its license plates. One could examine
Country's erasure of the various manifestations of difference, including class, within which community in South Berwick and its
environs actually took shape. Or one might compare community
in *Country* with the more class-divided communities portrayed by
other New England writers, including Alice Brown, or with the
prospect of cross-racial, cross-ethnic urban community suggested
by Alice Dunbar-Nelson's *The Goodness of St. Rocque* (1899), which
is set in New Orleans. If the possibilities for investigation are numerous, Jewett's own example suggests that pursuing the implications of any particular model of community has long been part of
American practice. Indeed, Americans' willingness to think critically and creatively about community remains vital to the endurance of community as a live concept and thus to the genuine
viability of the American nation itself.

NOTES

1. Sarah Orne Jewett, *The Country of the Pointed Firs and Other Stories*, ed.
   Mary Ellen Chase, intro. Marjorie Pryse (1896; rpt. New York: Nor-
   ton, 1982), p. 90. All citations are to this edition.
2. Good examples of informed appreciation include Elizabeth Ammons,
   *Conflicting Stories: American Women Writers at the Turn into the Twentieth
   Century* (New York: Oxford Univ. Press, 1991) and "Going in Circles:
   The Female Geography of Jewett's *Country of the Pointed Firs,*" *Studies in
   the Literary Imagination* 16, no. 2 (1983): 83–92; Sarah Way Sherman,
   Sarah Orne Jewett, an American Persephone (Hanover, N.H.: Univ. Press
   of New England, 1989); and Marjorie Pryse, Introduction to *The Coun-
   try of the Pointed Firs.* See also Sandra A. Zagarell, "Narrative of Community: The Identification of a Genre," in Vèvè A. Clark, Ruth-Ellen R.
   Joeres, and Madelon Sprengnether (eds.), *Revising the Word and the
   World: Essays in Feminist Literary Criticism* (Chicago: Univ. of Chicago
   Press, 1993), pp. 249–78. That scholarly work on Jewett has become
   more historically analytic of late is exemplified by Elizabeth Ammons's essay in this volume, which deftly explores some of the cultural politics of Jewett's representation of the world of Dunnet Landing.

3. The Bishop article, to which I am much indebted, appeared in the *New England Quarterly* 30, no. 2 (1957): 243–49. Werner Berthoff, "The Art of Jewett's *Pointed Firs,*" *New England Quarterly* 32, no. 1 (1959): 53; Josephine Donovan, *Sarah Orne Jewett* (New York: Ungar, 1980), esp. pp. 94–7; Sherman, *An American Persephone,* esp. pp. 48–9. In a recent discussion of Jewett's blurring of literary genres, Karen Oakes touches briefly on the questions of race and racial mixing in *Country.* See "'All That Lay Deepest in Her Heart": Reflections on Jewett, Gender, and Genre," *Colby Quarterly* 26 (1990): 152–60.

4. While these facts are so familiar as to need no particular citation, I acknowledge here my particular debt to two well-known studies for information about late-nineteenth-century American attitudes toward race and immigration: John Higham, *Strangers in the Land: Patterns of American Nativism, 1860–1925* (New Brunswick, N.J.: Rutgers Univ. Press, 1955), and Thomas F. Gossett, *Race: The History of an Idea in America* (Dallas, Tex.: Southern Methodist Univ. Press, 1963). For information about European concepts of race, I have found especially useful Martin Bernal, *Black Athena: The Afroasiatic Roots of Classical Civilization,* vol. 1: *The Fabrication of Ancient Greece, 1785–1985* (London: Free Association Books, 1987).

5. Jay Martin, *Harvests of Change: American Literature, 1865–1914* (Englewood Cliffs, N.J.: Prentice-Hall, 1967), p. 5.

6. Gossett, *Race,* p. 306. In an 1892 letter Aldrich told a friend, "I . . . wrote a misanthropic poem called 'Unguarded Gates' (July 'Atlantic'!) in which I mildly protest against America becoming the cesspool of Europe. . . . I believe in America for the Americans; . . . I hold that jail-birds, professional murderers, amateur lepers ('moon-eyed' or otherwise), and human gorillas generally should be closely questioned at our Gates'" (quoted in Ferris Greenslit, *The Life of Thomas Bailey Aldrich* [Boston: Houghton, Mifflin, 1908], pp. 168–9).

7. Gossett, *Race,* p. 311. Hyppolyte Taine, the French man of letters whose work influenced American writers such as Howells and Norris, considered literature to be an expression of race, historical moment, and milieu. His *History of English Literature* reads that literature as the manifestation of the predominant English racial trait, common sense.

8. Sarah Orne Jewett, *The Story of the Normans, Told Chiefly in Relation to Their Conquest of England* (New York: Putnam's; London, T. Fisher Unwin, 1886; rpt. 1890), p. 365, referred to as *SON* in my text. Of the Normans' adventuring spirit, Jewett also maintained that being a "crusader" was innate to the "Normans of the twelfth century" and asserted that "you find Englishmen of the same stamp" throughout

post-Conquest English history, citing Sir Walter Raleigh, Lord Nelson, Stanley and Dr. Livingston, and General Gordon.

9. Some of Jewett's letters also indicate that racial distinctions and belief in a racial hierarchy informed her political and social observations. One example is the reference to England's control over Ireland in an 1884 letter to her friend Annie Fields: "The two races were antagonistic. . . . Ireland is backward, and when she is equal to being independent, and free to make her own laws, I suppose the way will be opened, and she will be under grace of herself, instead of tutors and governors in England" (Annie Fields, ed., *Letters of Sarah Orne Jewett* [Boston: Houghton Mifflin, 1911], pp. 22–3).

10. Contemporary pronouncements about America's cultural purity like that of Barrett Wendell – "the greatness of New England letters in the period from 1830 to 1860 was to be attributed to the fact that the region was then almost racially homogeneous" (Gossett, *Race*, p. 134) – illuminate *Country's* emphasis on cultural uniformity as a delicate assertion of the need to preserve true "Americana" from contamination by difference or foreignness.

11. See my "Narrative of Community" for a more extensive discussion of this strain of fiction. The less historically and culturally analytic approach I have taken in that essay is consonant with my more celebratory attitude toward narrative of community in 1988.

12. Although, early in the century, "community" still referred to a specific demographic unit, the village, and most Americans still lived in such communities, by the post–Civil War era, as historian Thomas Bender suggests, the communities to which most Americans belonged were no longer simply local or even defined by place. Some aspects of community – the social, the affectional – tended to take shape in face-to-face or local circumstances, but others, especially the economic and political aspects, were organized in translocal networks. See Thomas Bender, *Community and Social Change in America* (New Brunswick, N.J.: Rutgers Univ. Press, 1978).

13. For examples see Ammons, Berthoff, Sherman, Zagarell, and also Marcia M. Folsom, " 'Tact Is a Kind of Mind-Reading': Empathic Style in Sarah Orne Jewett's *The Country of the Pointed Firs*," *Colby Library Quarterly* 18, no. 1 (1982): 66–78, and Joseph Allen Boone, *Tradition Counter Tradition: Love and the Forms of Fiction*, Women in Culture and Society Series, ed. Catharine R. Stimpson (Chicago: Univ. of Chicago Press, 1987).

14. In *Conflicting Stories*, Ammons explores the development of two quite different structural principles in *Country:* a linear plot that traces the

narrator's coming to terms with the kind of writing a subject like the Dunnet community requires and a weblike shape that constructs her relationship with Mrs. Todd.

15. Francis Otto Matthiesson, *Sarah Orne Jewett* (Boston: Houghton Mifflin, 1929), pp. 19–20. An important historical referent, the masts of the ships doomed by the embargo of 1803 to molder in the Dunnet harbor, though repressed throughout *Country,* emerges at the end, when the narrator looks back from the steamer to the town and sees "the tall masts of its disabled schooners in the inner bay" (p. 132).

16. "Race" and "family" had important similarities in nineteenth-century thought: Both were thought to be natural categories; the members of each were "related"; each had a traceable history and passed characteristics down through generations. Jewett's insistence on the kindred character of all nations that "descended" from the Northmen in *The Story of the Normans* exemplifies this kind of conflation.

17. Quoted by Gossett, *Race,* p. 291; the synopsis is Gossett's. Blaine conflates here the so-called old immigrants, groups whose members had been emigrating to the United States since antebellum days. Gossett takes this quotation from a book whose title is striking testimony, to late-twentieth-century ears, to the earlier respectability of a rhetoric that combined sexism and racism: Samuel Gompers and Herman Gutstadt's *Meat vs. Rice: American Manhood against Asiatic Coolieism, Which Shall Survive?* (San Francisco, 1908), p. 22.

18. Zagarell, "Narrative of Community," p. 273.

19. Formally articulated by the German sociologist Ferdinand Tönnies in his 1887 study *Gemeinschaft und Gesellschaft,* these ideas inform much Western social thought. See Robert A. Nisbet, *The Sociological Tradition* (New York: Basic Books, 1966), pp. 47–106, for a discussion of what he calls the "rediscovery of community" in the nineteenth century and its meanings in the systems of such social thinkers as Comte, Feuerbach, Marx, Tönnies, and Weber. The dichotomy between *Gemeinschaft* and *Gesellschaft* also tends to be rooted in a developmental model of history in which *Gemeinschaft* is associated with preindustrial life and *Gesellschaft* with modernity. Sociologist Joseph A. Gusfield gives a lucid explanation of this conflation in *Community: A Critical Response* (Oxford: Basil Blackwell, 1975).

20. See Zagarell, "Narrative of Community," pp. 269–71, for a discussion of the communal dimension of characterization in *Country.*

21. *Country's* distinction between its subject and its readers is characteristic of pastoral, with which it has often been associated. In a well-known formulation, William Empson maintains that pastoral is

59

"about" an audience whom it is not "by" or "for" (*Some Versions of Pastoral* [London: Chatto & Windus, 1935], p. 6).

22. Bernal, *Black Athena*, p. 348. From Matthew Arnold, *Culture and Anarchy* (London: Smith, Elder, 1869), p. 69. Bernal notes that "Britain had a philo-Semitic tradition which became particularly strong with the rise of the bourgeoisie in the mid-19th century" and that Arnold went to great lengths to identify this tradition as a consequence of the English civil war rather than coming from actual Semitic roots (see p. 347).

23. Richard Cary, ed., *Sarah Orne Jewett Letters*, rev. ed. (Waterville, Me.: Colby College Press, 1967), pp. 51–2.

24. Bernal, *Black Athena*, develops the identification of classical Greece with northern Europe in depth in chap. 5, "Romantic Linguistics," chap. 6, "Hellomania, I," and chap. 7, "Hellomania, II." He shows that, in the nineteenth century, Greece became identified as Caucasian. Classical scholars identified its original settlers as Caucasian, and the Caucasians were identified as a northern "race." Following a lineage like those according to which late-nineteenth-century Nordicists assigned Northern descent to Anglo-Saxons, Aryans, or other northern "races," *Country* positions Normans (originally, as Jewett says, "Northmen") as Greek descendants.

25. Alice Brown, Review of *The Country of the Pointed Firs*, in Gwen L. Nagel, ed., *Critical Essays on Sarah Orne Jewett* (Boston: Hall, 1984), pp. 37, 38. Reprinted from *Book Buyer* (New York) (October 1897): 249–50.

26. In the preface to her 1925 edition of *Country*, Cather identified this language as one reason for proclaiming *Country* one of three American books that "have the possibility of long life" (Sarah Orne Jewett, *Country of the Pointed Firs and Other Stories*, ed. Willa Cather [Garden City, N.Y.: Doubleday, n.d.], p. v).

27. Jewett's writing in the late 1890s suggests that she was of several minds about racial questions. A few of her stories, including "Between Now and Vespers" and "A Little Captive Maid" (both collected in *A Native of Winby and Other Tales*, 1893), are almost didactic in their resistance to the hatred of the Catholic Irish that plagued the nation, but at least one, "A War Debt" (collected in *The Life of Nancy*, 1895), casts African-Americans as inferior while valorizing Anglo-Normans of both North and South.

Gender and American Realism
in *The Country of the Pointed Firs*

MICHAEL DAVITT BELL

EVER since the publication of *The Country of the Pointed Firs* in 1896, Sarah Orne Jewett has been accorded a fairly consistent place in the American literary canon, although even her most enthusiastic partisans have felt compelled to insist that this place is very small. Thus Henry James, in a 1915 essay, describes the "minor compass" of Jewett's art and praises (if that is the right word) "her beautiful little quantum of achievement"; Willa Cather writes in a 1936 memoir that Jewett "was content to be slight, if she could be true"; Warner Berthoff, in a 1959 essay on *The Country of the Pointed Firs*, concludes that the book, "with a secure and unrivaled place in the main line of American literary expression," is "a small work but an unimprovable one."[1] Yet the consistency and endurance of Jewett's literary reputation, however hedged by diminutives, make her almost unique among American women fiction writers of the nineteenth century. And the place of *The Country of the Pointed Firs* in what Berthoff calls "the main line of American literary expression" has not simply depended on critical taste, at least not overtly; it has also been secured by the work's supposed location within the categories of official American literary history, the literary history that structures anthologies and academic curricula. Ever since William Dean Howells declared his so-called Realism War in the 1880s, only a decade before Jewett's book was published, a rugged commonplace of our literary history has been the notion that the great development in American fiction after the Civil War was the rise of realism. And as a supposed example of "local-color" fiction, of "regionalism," *The Country of the Pointed Firs* has conventionally been categorized as an expression of American realism.[2]

Associating Jewett with Howellsian realism makes a good deal of sense. "Don't try to write *about* people and things," her father early urged her, "tell them just as they are!"[3] — a piece of advice his daughter cherished and one that certainly sounds like the credo of a realist. Moreover, one of Jewett's first influential mentors in the public literary world was the very William Dean Howells who would lead the battle for literary realism in the 1880s and 1890s. In 1869, as assistant editor of the *Atlantic Monthly* (he became the editor in 1871), Howells accepted the first of the many stories Jewett would publish in that magazine, and his encouragement continued for the rest of her career. Jewett was one of the writers who led Howells to proclaim, in 1897, that in the United States "the sketches and studies by the women seem faithfuler and more realistic than those of the men," and he later praised her "incomparable sketches" for their "free movement, unfettered by the limits of plot, and keeping only to the reality."[4] Still, there are problems with classifying Jewett as a Howellsian realist — problems raised by her subject matter, her style, and perhaps above all (in spite of Howells's praise for women's stories) her gender, her status as a *woman* writer. These problems, quite closely interrelated, do not matter because of some inherent significance in the allocation of such labels as "realist." They matter, rather, because they point to issues and themes of considerable significance in *The Country of the Pointed Firs*. Reexamining the terms that have secured and sustained Jewett's place in the canon might help us understand why so many of her admirers have insisted on the supposedly diminutive dimensions of this place.

I

In 1885 William Dean Howells moved from Boston to New York to take on the "Editor's Study" column in *Harper's* magazine, and it was in these essays, selectively reissued as *Criticism and Fiction* in 1891, that he conducted his campaign for realism in American literature. One of the most interesting of the essays is a review (originally published in 1886) of Ulysses S. Grant's *Memoirs*. Modern criticism, Howells here contends, has "put a literary consciousness into books unfelt in the early masterpieces, but unfelt now only in the books of men whose lives have been passed in activities, who have been used to employing language as they would have employed any implement, to effect an object, who have regarded a thing to be said as in no wise different from a thing to be done"; Grant, we are assured, is just such a man. In Grant's *Memoirs*, Howells writes, "there is not a moment wasted in preening and prettifying, after the fashion of literary men; there is no thought of style, and so the style is good as it is in the Book of Chronicles, as it is in the Pilgrim's Progress, with a peculiar, almost plebeian, plainness at times." Here we see clearly the assumptions and values underlying Howells's thinking about literature, particularly the distinction, not between modes of literary representation ("realism," "romance," and the like), but between kinds of men. On the one side are artists, overwhelmed by "literary consciousness," concerned with "style"; on the other side are "real" men, "men whose lives have been passed in activities," and it is with this group that Howells seeks to ally himself. In an 1895 memoir, Howells describes his childhood recognition that "my reading gave me no standing among the boys, . . . with boys who were more valiant in fight or in play," and his subsequent discovery "that literature gives one no more certain station in the world of men's activities, either idle or useful." To put it bluntly and succinctly, literary realism mattered to Howells as an effort to suppress or overcome this discovery, to distinguish literary vocation, or at least realist literary vocation, from "criticism" and "style" – all this in order to present literature as *part* of the "world of men's activities."[5]

In this respect, American local-color fiction of the 1880s and 1890s – especially the New England local-color fiction produced by such women as Sarah Orne Jewett, Mary Wilkins Freeman, and Rose Terry Cooke – is the very antithesis of Howellsian realism. Jewett in fact wrote fiction dealing with a fairly wide variety of subjects and settings, including urban businessmen (and businesswomen), Irish and French Canadian immigrants, and the American Revolution, but she is now known almost entirely for her Maine local-color writing, most notably *The Country of the Pointed Firs*. And if realism sought to ally itself with the "world of men's activities," the characteristic world of New England local-color fiction is distinguished above all by the absence of men and masculine activity. The young and fit have fled this world for a reality that is always elsewhere, in the West or in the city, while those who remain, mostly women, maintain old proprieties and rituals whose function, like the men, seems long since to have vanished. Ann Douglas, in the title of an important essay, has called this women's local-color tradition a "literature of impoverishment," and the realism with which its world is portrayed only serves to underscore that what is absent from it is precisely the sort of reality to which writers like Howells wished to turn.[6]

Jewett's achievement, or at least the way it has come to be understood, also stands apart from Howells's strange but habitual denigration of "style" in literature, and such denigration was by no means a Howellsian idiosyncrasy. Frank Norris, for instance, wrote in 1899 that style "is precisely what I try most to avoid." "Who cares for fine style!" he added. "Tell your yarn and go to the devil. We don't want literature, we want life."[7] Jewett's reputation, by contrast, has had everything to do with attention to style. "Style has not been such a common phenomenon in America that its possessor can ever be ignored," writes F. O. Matthiessen at the end of his 1929 book on the author of The Country of the Pointed Firs; "Sarah Jewett," he continues, "realized its full importance." Or as Willa Cather puts it in her 1936 memoir: "Among fifty thousand books you will find very few writers who ever achieved a style at all. The distinctive thing about Miss Jewett is that she had an individual voice. . . . If you can . . . go to a quiet spot and take up a volume of Miss Jewett, you will find the voice still there, with a quality which any ear trained in literature must recognize."[8] Cather's insistence on the rare quality of "style," and her grounding proper appreciation of Jewett on training "in literature," could not more clearly distinguish her sense of Jewett's achievement from the ideas of such realists or naturalists as Howells and Norris.

At the heart of this distinction, it should be clear by now, are ingrained assumptions about gender, assumptions that in effect prohibited women from full participation in the realist program. Howells values the world of *men's* activities, and he dismisses care for style as a species of "preening and prettifying," a matter of "fashion" – as, in short, effeminate. Some of the implications of this kind of thinking can be seen in an astonishing essay by Frank Norris, "Why Women Should Write the Best Novels" – "and," so its title as a 1901 magazine article adds, "Why They Don't." According to Norris, women should write the best novels because they have leisure and a literary rather than a business education. Even more important, he insists, is what he sees as a fundamental difference of temperament separating women from men:

> The average man is a rectangular, square-cut, matter-of-fact, sober-minded animal who does not receive impressions easily, who is not troubled with emotions and has no overmastering desire to communicate his sensations to anybody. But the average woman is just the reverse of all these. She is impressionable, emotional, and communicative. And impressionableness, emotionality, and communicativeness are three very important qualities of mind that make for novel writing.

Why, then, do women *not* write the best novels? First of all, says Norris, trotting out his favorite aphorism, because "life is more important than literature"; and women, he writes, have little knowledge of "life itself," of "the crude, the raw, the vulgar," which constitute, for Norris, "real life." Women are also, he insists, physiologically and temperamentally incapable of serious literary exertion; he thus points to "the make-up of the woman," to the supposed "fact that protracted labour of the mind tells upon a woman quicker than upon a man." A man, he writes, "may grind on steadily for an almost indefinite period, when a woman at the same task would begin, after a certain point, to 'feel her nerves,' to chafe, to fret, to try to do too much, to polish too highly, to develop more perfectly. Then come fatigue, harassing doubts, more nerves, a touch of hysteria occasionally, exhaustion, and in the end complete discouragement and a final abandonment of the enterprise."[9]

Such ideas are blatantly, perhaps even laughably, compensatory, but for this very reason they served an important purpose for male writers who worried that being "literary" might compromise their masculinity.[10] These ideas have also no doubt played a role in the formation of Sarah Orne Jewett's somewhat peculiar literary reputation. She certainly did care for style, but one suspects the critical attention that has been paid to this concern (hardly a surprising concern, one would think, for a writer) has owed more than a little to the fact that Jewett was a woman. According to realist orthodoxy, after all, "style" is "feminine." And what about the bizarre but persistent critical interest in the *size* of Jewett's place in the canon? Here is Norris in 1896 (the year *The Country of the Pointed Firs* was published), praising the father of French naturalism:

> To be noted of M. Zola we must leave the rank and the file, either turn to the forefront of the marching world, or fall by the roadway. . . . The world of M. Zola is a world of big things; the enormous, the formidable, the terrible, is [*sic*] what counts; no teacup tragedies here.[11]

If the masculine ("marching") world of Zola is a "world of big things," as distinguished from the feminized world of "teacup tragedies," then *of course* the place accorded a woman writer in the main line of American literary expression would be bound to be small, a kind of respite from "the enormous, the formidable, the terrible." "Your voice," Howells wrote to Jewett in 1891, "is like a thrush's in the din of all the literary noises that stun us so."[12] This kind of thinking, moreover, has been as characteristic of women as of men; Cather, we recall, recommends that the reader who wants to appreciate Jewett's distinctive voice should "go to a quiet spot" before taking up one of her volumes.

II

The heavily gendered assumptions at the heart of American realist thinking have surely had much to do with what official literary history has made of Jewett, but there may be a more interesting way to approach the relation of American realism to *The Country of the Pointed Firs*. Instead of asking what American realism made of Jewett, we might ask what Jewett made of American realism — of the ideas of Howells and others about the "reality" of "men's activities." While Jewett did not expound on Howells's ideas in letters and prefaces, in aesthetic manifestos, we still might ask what attitudes are expressed or implied in her masterpiece. One way of answering this question is to say that Jewett, in *The Country of the Pointed Firs*, quite deliberately and completely turns Howellsian realism on its head, reversing or undercutting its deepest ambitions and assumptions. I will ultimately disagree with this answer, or at least qualify it to a significant degree, but it certainly has a strong and plausible appeal. The programs of Howells and Norris endorse a movement from the less to the more "real," from the feminine world of "teacup tragedies" to the "marching world," the "world of men's activities." *The Country of the Pointed Firs* seems to reverse this movement while retaining the valuation; here it is a movement *out* of the "world of men's activities" that appears to lead into a more intense "reality."

Think, for instance, about the portrayal of male characters in *The Country of the Pointed Firs*. Most of the men have died long ago, like Mrs. Todd's father and her husband, and the few male survivors of the old days are aptly represented by Captain Littlepage, who visits the narrator in the schoolhouse to which she retreats to pursue her writing and whose diminutive name already undermines the emphasis of writers like Norris on masculine bigness. "It was a dog's life," he says of the old days at sea, "but it made men of those who followed it" (p. 20) [13] – the point being, of course, that these man-making days are long past. The town doctor seems to maintain true authority, functioning in effect as Almira Todd's professional colleague, but he never really appears in the book; he is mentioned only a few times in passing. More typical is the minister, Mr. Dimmick, with whom Mrs. Todd remembers having sailed to visit "poor Joanna" Todd on Shell-heap Island. Against Mrs. Todd's protests, he insisted on tying the sheet to a cleat (the rope hurt his delicate hands), and when the wind rose he jumped up in panic and cried for help. "I knocked him right over into the bottom o' the bo't," she recalls, "getting by to catch hold of the sheet an' untie it." "He wasn't but a little man," this large woman continues; "I helped him right up after the squall passed, and made a handsome apology to him, but he did act kind o' offended" (p. 70). Mrs. Todd also recalls that later, when Mr. Dimmick took an accusatory tone with Joanna, "she didn't take no notice," instead showing him some Indian remains, "same's if he was a boy" (p. 75). Or there is old Santin Bowden, who organizes the line of march at the family reunion. A "soldierly little figure of a man," he is obsessed with matters military. We soon learn, however, that he was rejected for service in the Civil War – "He ain't a sound man," Mrs. Todd explains, "and they wouldn't have him" (p. 101) – and his dreams of military glory are only an empty parody of genuine manhood. "His life's all in it," says Mrs. Todd, "but he will have these poor gloomy spells come over him now an' then, an' then he has to drink" (p. 102). And when Mrs. Todd takes the narrator to visit Mrs. Blackett on Green Island, she has a clear reason for preferring to make the trip in a small boat: "We don't want to carry no men folks," she explains, "havin' to be considered every minute an' takin' up all our time" (p. 32).

Two male characters in The Country of the Pointed Firs, the old fisherman Elijah Tilley and Mrs. Todd's brother William, are exempted from this general dismissal – largely, it seems, because they have in many respects become "feminine." Elijah Tilley, a widower for the past eight years, is still unconsoled over the loss of his "poor dear." In fair weather he fishes, but in winter he occupies himself with knitting. "Mother," he explains, "learnt me once when I was a lad; she was a beautiful knitter herself" (p. 125). William Blackett, an aging bachelor, has chosen to stay on Green Island with his mother. He is almost pathologically shy, he is "son and daughter both" to Mrs. Blackett (p. 41), and when the narrator finally meets him she notes that he looks "just like his mother" (p. 44). According to Mrs. Todd, who takes after her father, William is in spite of his maternal resemblance even less masculine than Mrs. Blackett. "He ought," she says, "to have made something o' himself, bein' a man an' so like mother; but though he's been very steady to work, an' kept up the farm, an' done his fishin' too right along, he never had mother's snap an' power o' seein' things just as they be" (p. 47).

When Captain Littlepage visits the narrator's schoolhouse, he tells her a story he heard from a man named Gaffett, whom he met when he was shipwrecked and stranded on the shores of Hudson's Bay with winter setting in. Gaffett claimed to be the sole survivor of a polar expedition (recalling the southern voyage in Poe's Narrative of Arthur Gordon Pym) that discovered "a strange sort of a country 'way up north beyond the ice, and strange folks living in it." From a distance the place looked like any other town, but it was inhabited by silent "blowing gray figures," "fog-shaped men" who vanished when approached "like a leaf the wind takes with it, or a piece of cobweb." The explorers believed this to be "a kind of waiting-place between this world an' the next" (pp. 24–6). The captain's story, with which he has become obsessed, is dismissed by his neighbors as the raving of an unbalanced mind, but this "waiting place" might strike one as a pertinent and somber analogue of Dunnet Landing itself, stranded in northern isolation, populated mainly by relics of its own lost past. The narrator is quite aware of this potential analogy; later, when Mrs. Todd offers her a mug of root beer, she feels "as if my enchantress would now begin to look like the cobweb shapes of the arctic town" (p. 31).

Still, what seems to matter most about Gaffett's "waiting-place" is that it is a community of fog-shaped *men*, an image of failed *male* power, and Dunnet Landing, by contrast, is a community of *women*, presided over by Almira Todd and her universally beloved mother. This is the reality Jewett seems to substitute for the compensatory masculinity of writers like Howells and Norris. Mrs. Todd appears to possess an almost magical power over nature; for instance, when she twitches the sheet on the way to Green Island, "as if she urged the wind like a horse," the elements oblige: "There came at once a fresh gust, and we seemed to have doubled our speed" (p. 35). Immediately following the story of Gaffett's "waiting-place," the narrator's first sight of Green Island from the shore produces something like an effect of apotheosis:

> It had been growing gray and cloudy, like the first evening of autumn, and a shadow had fallen on the darkening shore. Suddenly, as we looked, a gleam of golden sunshine struck the outer islands, and one of them shone out clear in the light, and revealed itself in a compelling way to our eyes. . . . The sunburst on that outermost island made it seem like a sudden revelation of the world beyond this which some believe to be so near.
>
> "That's where mother lives," said Mrs. Todd. (p. 30)

It is only fitting that the *female* "world beyond this," the world "where mother lives," be *Green* Island, its fertility standing in contrast to the polar grayness of Gaffett's realm of fog-shaped men. So, too, the true center of authority at the Bowden family reunion is not Sant Bowden – whose military posturing nicely deflates, for instance, Frank Norris's fantasy of the "marching world" – but Mrs. Blackett. As Mrs. Todd puts it, shortly after the crowd has been described as resembling "bees . . . swarming in the lilac bushes," "Mother's always the queen" (p. 98). In this matriarchal world, it would seem, the men can only be drones.

The most interesting recent discussions of *The Country of the Pointed Firs*, inspired by developments in feminist criticism, have rejected the notion of the impoverishment of its female characters, stressing instead the book's celebration of women's experience and women's communities, and even its cultivation of distinctively female styles and modes of narrative.[14] For instance, Marjorie Pryse, drawing on Adrienne Rich's *Of Woman Born*, writes that the "lost world" of the book "is not the world of shipping, but a world in which women were once united with their mothers and inherited their mothers' powers." Jewett, she argues, "does not share the literary historians' fiction of a New England in decline," and "the apparent loss of male paradise in the American literary imagination in the years following the American Civil War simply serves as a contrast to the fecundity and depth of imagination in Jewett and her female contemporaries." Thus "the world of Dunnet Landing is," for Pryse, "above all else, a world in which women learn to belong again. . . . *Pointed Firs* reminds us that there still exists a country – and a world – where the vision of women is not only vital, but can be shared."[15] In a similar vein Elizabeth Ammons, drawing on Carol Gilligan's *In a Different Voice*, finds behind Jewett's rejection of masculine, linear plot an alternative structure relying on "essentially female psychic patterns," patterns of "web" and "descent." The experience expressed in *The Country of the Pointed Firs*, Ammons writes, is "not grounded in separation and aggression but in connection, in feelings of intimate relatedness to others."[16]

Readings like these, rejecting the idea that women's local-color writing is inherently impoverished, help us recognize aspects of *The Country of the Pointed Firs* that had earlier seemed, at best, indistinct and blurred.[17] They also attribute to the book something it has surely never before been seen as having – a polemical or even political intention – and it is to this idea of the book's polemical intention that I devote the rest of this essay. Just what sort of feminist point, it seems appropriate to ask, is being attributed to *The Country of the Pointed Firs;* what sort of power is Jewett supposed to be claiming for her powerful women characters? Or, to raise a somewhat different question, to what extent do these new readings of *The Country of the Pointed Firs* overcome the way Jewett has been placed and marginalized in the main line of an American literary history defined largely in terms of masculine (or masculinist?) "realism"? Here, paradoxically, one is compelled to recognize that these new readings may tend less to overcome than to perpetuate this marginalization.

III

In his 1959 essay on *The Country of the Pointed Firs,* Warner Berthoff contends that Jewett's women, women deserted by men, exemplify "distorted, repressed, unfulfilled or transformed sexuality" and that for these women "the only choice, the sacrifice required for survival, is to give up a woman's proper life and cover the default of the men."[18] It is hard to share Berthoff's assumptions about what is normal or proper for women, or to imagine that Jewett shared them; she, after all, never married and never wished to, and the major emotional relationships of her life were with other women — most notably, from the early 1880s on, with Annie Fields of Boston.[19] But it may be equally hard to find any other clear position on "woman's proper life" in *The Country of the Pointed Firs.* Again and again the reader confronts disparities between what the women of Dunnet Landing seem to represent and the actual circumstances of their lives.

Marjorie Pryse writes of the "fecundity and depth of imagination in Jewett and her female contemporaries," and images of fecundity are repeatedly associated, in *The Country of the Pointed Firs,* with Almira Todd, with her mother, and with Mrs. Blackett's refuge on Green Island.[20] But on what literal reality, we should ask, are such images based? Mrs. Blackett may be the "queen," but she has long ago passed the years of childbearing, and her daughter had no children nor, apparently, did Elijah Tilley and his "poor dear." Fecundity, in the world of Dunnet Landing, is conveyed wholly through images and metaphors — Pryse is exactly right to refer to fecundity "of imagination" — and these are images, as well, of plants and flowers. There are no visible signs here of human or even animal reproduction; such things, in a world where "children" like William and Almira have reached advanced middle age, are as much in the past as the days of shipping. There are young children at the Bowden family reunion, but their presence is registered only as a brief intrusion. Mrs. Todd's "great grief and silence," we are told in Chapter 10, stand in marked contrast to the "noisy world" (p. 49); in this context the "chattering crowd of noisy children" at the reunion (p. 99) is linked not with Dunnet Landing but with the outside world – just as the narrator finds even Dunnet Landing, when she returns from her visit to Green Island, "large and noisy and oppressive" (p. 55).

Both Pryse and Ammons observe that the women in *The Country of the Pointed Firs,* unlike the male characters, are associated with belonging, with community, and there can be no doubt of the truth and importance of this observation. But it, too, can be exaggerated. What makes the Bowden family reunion memorable, after all, is the fact of its being a rare occurrence, an annual respite from what is mainly a life of isolation and solitude. Although she has an innate gift of hospitality, Mrs. Blackett lives almost alone on a remote island, and her daughter Almira, surely the book's principal representative of its women's community, also – and in some essential way – lives alone. "There was something lonely and solitary about her great determined shape," the narrator writes in Chapter 10; "she might have been Antigone alone on the Theban plain" (p. 49). And in the final chapter, as Mrs. Todd walks away before the narrator's departure, her distant figure looks "mateless and appealing, with something about it that was strangely self-possessed and mysterious" (p. 131). Here again, actual circumstances seem to be at odds with symbolic "women's values."

Berthoff writes that Captain Littlepage's story is "in some ways . . . the boldest and most decisive passage in the book, for it secures that reference to the life of male action and encounter without which the narrator's sympathy for backwater Dunnet would seem myopic, sentimental."[21] It is a little difficult to see what is supposed to be bold or decisive about this tale of intangible fog creatures, except for the fact that it is told by men and about men, and maybe this is the point, so that we see once more the careful distinction between Jewett's "backwater" world and the masculine mainstream of American realism – like Howells's distinction between Jewett's thrushlike voice and the "din of all the literary noises that stun us so." Here, however, we should recognize that the new feminist readings of *The Country of the Pointed Firs*, although they disagree with Berthoff's valuation, generally retain the terms of his distinction. Ammons, for instance, writes that *The Country of the Pointed Firs* "turns its back on the competitive world of men, literally leaving cantankerous Boston miles behind, and explores the quiet affectional realm of women."²² Berthoff and Ammons agree, albeit with different emphases and agendas, that the culture of women exists somehow outside the competitive culture of men, and this similarity should probably not surprise us. Jewett herself, we recall, distinguishes Almira Todd's "grief and silence" from the "noisy world."

But while the underlying similarity between Berthoff's "backwater" and Ammons's "quiet affectional realm" should not surprise us, perhaps it ought to trouble us a bit. To focus exclusively on what we might call the communal or separatist feminism of *The Country of the Pointed Firs* seems inevitably to perpetuate the gendered terms of realist thinking – even, in many respects, as that thinking is represented by so foolish a figure as Frank Norris. Such a focus obscures, too, a rather different sort of feminism also at work in the book, one that might help explain the disparity between what the women of Dunnet Landing seem to represent and the actual circumstances of their lives. Following her account of the trip to Green Island, for example, the narrator turns to the visit she and Mrs. Todd received from Mrs. Fosdick, a visit whose centerpiece is the story of Mrs. Todd's cousin by marriage, "poor Joanna." Years before the narrator's sojourn in Dunnet Landing, Joanna Todd was jilted by her fiancé, and she moved out to Shell-heap Island to live and die alone; she was, as Mrs. Todd puts it, "done with the world" (p. 76). Joanna's retreat from "the world" bears an intriguing resemblance to the narrator's own retreat from the city to Dunnet Landing, and Mrs. Todd seems to recognize this resemblance; among the presents she leaves for the narrator at the end of the book is the coral pin that Nathan Todd, years before, had bought for Joanna. Joanna's withdrawal, it should be clear, is less an expression of personal sorrow than an act of protest, even defiance. "I've done the only thing I could do," she told Almira, "and

I've made my choice. . . . I was in great wrath and trouble, and my thoughts was so wicked towards God that I can't expect ever to be forgiven" (p. 76). She did not, this is to say, seek forgiveness; she remained true to her anger. According to Mrs. Fosdick, Joanna "thought she wasn't fit to live with anybody, and wanted to be free" (p. 65); Joanna's story leads the narrator to reflect "upon a state of society which admitted such personal freedom and a voluntary hermitage" (p. 69). This may seem a severely restricted sort of freedom, but that is of course the point: Joanna makes her "choice," ironically but inevitably, by doing "the only thing I could do."

"In a wider sphere," the narrator writes of Mrs. Fosdick, "one might have called her a woman of the world . . . , but Mrs. Todd's wisdom was an intimation of truth itself" (p. 59). Almira Todd, for the worldly and apparently world-weary narrator, is the antithesis of "the world"; she is a kind of primal essence. We might wonder, however, if this sort of valorization bears any relation to the way Mrs. Todd sees herself, and we ought to pay attention to what we learn about the story of her life. When the narrator tells Mrs. Blackett that "it was impossible not to wish to stay on forever at Green Island," Mrs. Blackett agrees but adds that Almira would have been "very restless" if she had stayed, since she "wanted more scope" (p. 52). So Almira, as a child, was sent to Dunnet Landing to stay with an aunt and go to school, presumably at the very same schoolhouse the narrator is now renting in order to pursue the solitary and worldly career of literature. And even the apparently sentimental tale of Almira's hopeless love for "one who was far above her" (p. 7), in some ways similar to the story of Joanna's jilting, may matter less as a love story than as another example of Mrs. Todd's restlessness, of her desire for scope, for "the world." What has happened in her story, clearly, is that this desire has been frustrated.

The Country of the Pointed Firs, Marjorie Pryse insists, "portrays a world in which women are alone but not tragic."[23] It is certainly true that the absence of men from this world is not presented as a tragedy for Jewett's women, but Mrs. Todd does remind the narrator of "Antigone alone on the Theban plain," and there surely *is* something tragic about the absence for these women of the freedom and scope that have enabled the men to *become* absent. In the social bustle of the Bowden reunion, the narrator comes to recognize that "sometimes when Mrs. Todd had seemed limited and heavily domestic, she had simply grown sluggish for lack of proper surroundings"; "it was not the first time," she continues, "that I was full of wonder at the waste of human ability in this world. . . . More than one face among the Bowdens showed that only opportunity and stimulus were lacking, – a narrow set of circumstances had caged a fine able character and held it captive" (pp. 105–7). The narrator's recognition that Almira Todd has been caged by narrow circumstances, that her worldly ambitions have been frustrated, does not undercut our sense of Mrs. Todd's primal power, nor does it ironize the affirmation of the ideal of women's community represented by Mrs. Todd and her mother. But it does reveal that a price has been paid for the isolation of these qualities in places like Dunnet Landing.

What this isolation suggests about Jewett's relation to Howellsian realism is, in the last analysis, somewhat complicated. In the most obvious sense, realist thinking would seem simply irrelevant to Jewett; she surely had no need to downplay style and the literary in order to present herself as a "real" man, and the portraits of the minister Dimmick and Sant Bowden reveal an amused scorn for men with such needs. It is thus tempting to see Jewett as presenting a radical alternative to what Howells called the "world of men's activities," an alternative secured through removal, through withdrawal from the world; and such withdrawal – from the city to Dunnet Landing, or from Dunnet Landing to Green Island and the Bowden reunion – does constitute the main action of *The Country of the Pointed Firs*. Yet the stories of Almira Todd and Joanna (and, perhaps, the androgyny of the latter's name, combining "Joe" and "Anna") seem to suggest a counterimpulse, albeit a frustrated one: a desire to move *out* of the world of Dunnet Landing and *into* the "world of men's activities." Should we see here, then, a kind of secret, frustrated connection to the ideological underpinnings of Howellsian realism?

The answer to this question is no – for reasons revealed, for instance, in a story told by Mrs. Fosdick. The chapter in which she first appears is entitled "A Strange Sail," and Mrs. Fosdick is consistently associated with the supposedly masculine realm of sea travel rather than the quiet community of women. Soon after her arrival, she describes having gone to sea with her whole family, when she was eight years old. She wore her brother's clothes, since her own had inadvertently been left at home. As soon as the ship reached a port, her mother went ashore to purchase proper "feminine" attire, but they did not reach port for some time. "So I had quite a spell o' freedom," Mrs. Fosdick concludes.

> Mother made my new skirt long because I was growing, and I poked about the deck after that, real discouraged, feeling the hem at my heels every minute, and as if youth was past and gone. I liked the trousers best; I used to climb the riggin' with 'em and frighten mother till she said an' vowed she'd never take me to sea again. (p. 61)

We should pay careful attention to the meaning of cross-dressing in this brief story. Mrs. Fosdick's fondness for trousers had nothing to do with wanting to be masculine or wanting to be *with* men. What she regrets, rather, is her loss of freedom, and this freedom is a masculine quality only in the sense that in her world it is denied to women.

Mrs. Fosdick's regret over her loss of freedom may help explain her fascination with the story of "poor Joanna," but she is by no means consumed with regret, and soon after telling the story of her sea voyage this seasoned traveler is commenting on the sociable pleasures of "old acquaintance" – since, as she puts it, "conversation's got to have some roots in the past" (p. 61). The truth is that Jewett's women in *The Country of the Pointed Firs* are at the same time rooted *and* restless, enriched *and* impoverished, sustained by domestic routine *and* frustrated by it. While they experience a genuine sense of communal sharing they also, in Mrs. Fosdick's wonderful domestic image, feel the hem at their heels every minute. In contrast to the view of a reader like Warner Berthoff, Jewett's own view of her characters is not at all pathological; she does not, from the perspective of what I have been calling realist thinking, regard the lives of her solitary women as *abnormal*. But she does recognize the limitations that hem these lives in: limitations imposed by, among other things, the norms – the assumptions about "reality" and about the gendered allocation of different "realities" – that underlay the literary ideas of men like Howells and Norris. *The Country of the Pointed Firs* does not finally force either/or distinctions; and it may be this quality, above all, that separates the book from the discourse of American realism, with its rigid bifurcation of "literature" and "life," "teacup tragedies" and the "world of men's activities." We should resist the impulse to reimpose these bifurcations on *The Country of the Pointed Firs,* even in the interest of finding in it an *inversion* of realist values. The book itself is capable of affirming its community of women without conspiring in the assumption that women should inevitably be hemmed and marginalized. And its elegiac celebration of the world of Dunnet Landing still contains at least an undercurrent of protest against a climate in which women like Joanna must make their choices by doing the only thing they can do.

NOTES

1. Henry James, "Mr. and Mrs. James T. Fields," rpt. in *Henry James: Literary Criticism – Essays on Literature, American Writers, English Writers* (New York: Library of America, 1984), p. 174; Willa Cather, "Miss Jewett," in *Not Under Forty* (New York: Knopf, 1936), p. 89; Werner Berthoff, "The Art of Jewett's *Pointed Firs*" (1959), rpt. in *Fictions and Events: Essays in Criticism and Literary History* (New York: Dutton, 1971), p. 263. Cather's 1936 essay incorporates most of the preface she wrote in 1925 for *The Best Stories of Sarah Orne Jewett,* but it drops the final two paragraphs, including the claim that *The Country of the Pointed Firs, The Scarlet Letter,* and *Huckleberry Finn* are the "three American books which have the possibility of a long, long life" (rpt. in *The Country of the Pointed Firs and Others Stories* [Garden City, N.Y.: Doubleday, 1956], p. 11). For a provocative recent discussion of Jewett's supposedly "minor" status and ambitions, including an epilogue on *The Country of the Pointed Firs,* see Louis A. Renza, *"A White Heron" and the Question of Minor Literature* (Madison: Univ. of Wisconsin Press, 1984).

2. For characteristic examples of this inclusion of regional and local-color writing within the "larger" current of realism see the section "Regionalism, Local-Color Realism" in Warner Berthoff's *The Ferment of Realism: American Literature, 1884–1919* (New York: Free Press,

1965), pp. 90–103, and Eric Sundquist's chapter, "Realism and Regionalism," in Emory Elliot, ed., *Columbia Literary History of the United States* (New York: Columbia Univ. Press, 1988), pp. 501–24.

3. Quoted by Jewett in "Looking Back on Girlhood," *Youth's Companion* 65 (January 7, 1892): 6.

4. *Criticism and Fiction and Other Essays by W. D. Howells*, ed. Clara Marburg Kirk and Rudolf Kirk (New York: New York Univ. Press, 1959), pp. 64, 194.

5. Ibid., p. 26; William Dean Howells, *My Literary Passions* (New York: Harper & Brothers, 1895), p. 26. I have discussed this aspect of Howells's thinking about literature in "The Sin of Art and the Problem of American Realism: William Dean Howells," *Prospects* 9 (1985): 115–42.

6. Ann Douglas, "The Literature of Impoverishment: The Women Local Colorists in America, 1865–1914," *Women's Studies* 1 (1972): 2–40. Douglas contrasts what she sees as the impoverishment of local-color writers with the ambitions and successful careers of the so-called sentimental women writers of the 1850s and 1860s. Most literary historians, however, contrast the supposed minor scope of local-color fiction with the work of contemporaneous white, male "realists." As Eric Sundquist puts it: "Economic or political power can itself be seen to be definitive of a realist aesthetic, in that those in power (say, white urban males) have more often been judged 'realists,' while those removed from the seats of power (say, Midwesterners, blacks, immigrants, or women) have been categorized as regionalists" ("Realism and Regionalism," p. 503). Also see chap. 1, "'A White Heron' as a Maine Current," in Renza's *"A White Heron" and the Question of Minor Literature*, pp. 43–72.

7. *The Letters of Frank Norris*, ed. Franklin Walker (San Francisco: Book Club of California, 1956), pp. 30–1. I have discussed Norris's literary ideas and their relation to Howells's in "Frank Norris, Style, and the Problem of American Naturalism," *Studies in the Literary Imagination* 19, no. 2 (Fall 1983): 93–106.

8. F. O. Matthiessen, *Sarah Orne Jewett* (Boston: Houghton Mifflin, 1919), p. 148; Cather, *Not Under Forty*, p. 95.

9. *The Complete Works of Frank Norris* (Garden City, N.Y.: Doubleday, 1928), vol. 7, pp. 178–9, 181.

10. For a somewhat different argument along these lines see Alfred Habegger, *Gender, Fantasy, and Realism in American Literature* (New York: Columbia Univ. Press, 1982).

11. *The Literary Criticism of Frank Norris,* ed. Donald Pizer (Austin: University of Texas Press, 1964), p. 72.
12. *Life in Letters of William Dean Howells,* ed. Mildred Howells (Garden City, N.Y.: Doubleday, Doran, 1928), vol. 2, p. 15.
13. All parenthetical page references are to *The Country of the Pointed Firs and Other Stories,* ed. Mary Ellen Chase, intro. Marjorie Pryse (New York: Norton, 1982).
14. This position puts its proponents in direct opposition, for instance, to the argument of Ann Douglas. The local colorists' "theme," Douglas insists, is not "that of female superiority. It is not that their women are not superior to their men: more often than not, they are. But the important and painful fact which their literature underscores is that women, whether superior or inferior, are superfluous as individuals, and strangely superannuated as a sex." The local colorists, Douglas writes, "valued . . . the conventional feminine virtues, but they had lost faith in their potency" ("The Literature of Impoverishment," pp. 17, 16).
15. Marjorie Pryse, "Introduction to the Norton Edition," in *The Country of the Pointed Firs and Other Stories,* ed. Chase, pp. xiii, xix.
16. Elizabeth Ammons, "Going in Circles: The Female Geography of Jewett's *Country of the Pointed Firs,*" *Studies in the Literary Imagination* 16, no. 2 (Fall 1983): 83–84. See Ammons's *Conflicting Stories: American Women Writers at the Turn into the Twentieth Century* (New York: Oxford Univ. Press, 1991) for a revised version of this discussion.
17. See, too, Julia Bader, "The Dissolving Vision: Realism in Jewett, Freeman, and Gilman," in Eric J. Sundquist, ed., *American Realism: New Essays* (Baltimore: Johns Hopkins Univ. Press, 1982), pp. 176–98, and Sarah Way Sherman, *Sarah Orne Jewett, an American Persephone* (Hanover, N.H.: Univ. Press of New England, 1989), esp. pp. 196–235.
18. Berthoff, *Fictions and Events,* p. 250.
19. On this matter, see especially Josephine Donovan, "The Unpublished Love Poems of Sarah Orne Jewett," *Frontiers: A Journal of Women Studies* 4, no. 3 (1979): 26–31 (rpt. in Gwen L. Nagel, ed., *Critical Essays on Sarah Orne Jewett* [Boston: Hall, 1984], pp. 107–17) and chap. 4 (pp. 69–90) of Sherman's *Sarah Orne Jewett, an American Persephone.*
20. Elizabeth Ammons glosses a particularly resonant image evoked in Chapter 10, "Where Pennyroyal Grew." Here the narrator helps gather that herb on Green Island, where it grows, Mrs. Todd says, as it

grows nowhere else in the world. Pennyroyal, Ammons explains, "is used in childbirth to promote the expulsion of the placenta; it is also . . . an agent used to induce or increase menstrual flow. Thus . . . pennyroyal suggests maternal power itself: the central awesome power of women, like the Earth, to give or not to give life" ("Going in Circles," p. 91).

21. Berthoff, *Fictions and Events*, p. 254.
22. Ammons, "Going in Circles," p. 84.
23. Pryse, "Introduction to the Norton Edition," p. xix.

4

Material Culture, Empire, and Jewett's *Country of the Pointed Firs*

ELIZABETH AMMONS

A T the end of *The Country of the Pointed Firs* a number of Bowden reunioners eat "a model of the old Bowden house made of durable gingerbread."[1] They have already devoured an assortment of pies on which "dates and names" have been "wrought in lines of pastry and frosting on the tops." Then, as the narrator explains: "There was even more elaborate reading matter on an excellent early-apple pie which we began to share and eat, precept upon precept. Mrs. Todd helped me generously to the whole word *Bowden,* and consumed *Reunion* herself" (p. 108). This feast of language near the end of Jewett's text is very important in a book about a modern woman writer finding renewal and nurture in a matrifocal community. The consumption of words baked and frosted by women fuses the realms of literary art (language) and domestic arts (cooking); it says that connection, rather than division, is possible between ambitious modern women writers and their maternal forebears.[2] But why do they eat the house?

One way to think about *The Country of the Pointed Firs* is as a material history. From this point of view, Jewett's story seeks to recover and understand the past through serious contemplation and representation of the texts of daily life: the objects, structures, rituals, and landscapes that people shape and are shaped by. Rather than search tomes and archives to create history, the material culturalist goes into the field and examines the ordinary artifacts of daily life. Material history, as Robert Blair St. George puts it, is "in general terms, a history more about daily routine than about exceptional deeds, more about common houses, fences, and fields than about country estates and Copley portraits."[3] It is a history that, like Jewett's *Country of the Pointed Firs,* is concerned with reading and interpreting the material objects and rituals of a specific time and place. "Things" become "whole texts, each one an objectification of thought, a concrete enactment of morality, an eloquent essay in the difficult reconciliation of ethics, aesthetics, and economics."[4] The task for the material culturalist is to read and interpret – the two acts being inseparable in the apprehension of any text – furniture, food, architecture, clothes, art objects, festivals, and ceremonies in order to create from those texts a new text, the one we read and interpret. The announced goal of this intellectual production is to offer a truthful and persuasive version of past life in a region as ordinarily experienced by ordinary inhabitants. A less obvious goal, however, is the one that interests me here, and it has to do with the present. (Since Jewett chooses fiction as her medium, this goal is in certain ways quite apparent in her work.) The material culturalist uses old texts to make a new one that serves some purpose in the present by promoting one particular version of the past as opposed to some other version or versions.

As the gobbling of the Bowden house at the reunion suggests, two of the important material texts considered in *The Country of the Pointed Firs* are houses and ritual feasts. Indeed, in her literary text about these material texts Jewett, through her narrator, invites us to join the final feast and eat the house. As readers consuming the text of *The Country of the Pointed Firs,* which lies in our hands, we mimic the wolfing of words and of re-created material texts that constitutes the communal sacrament at the end of Jewett's narrative. Just as the consumed house in the narrator's text is a baked version of a "real" physical structure, so the consumable text in our hands, the book we are "eating," is an artistically rendered version or re-presentation of a supposedly "real" place and set of events. This brings me back to my initial question: When we take communion with Jewett, her narrator, Mrs. Todd, and the rest at the end of *The Country of the Pointed Firs* – when we eat the word and swallow the house – what are we celebrating?

The opening sentence of *The Country of the Pointed Firs* focuses attention on material environment. "There was something about the coast town of Dunnet which made it seem more attractive than

other maritime villages of eastern Maine" (p. 1). This emphasis on
the visual pleasure the narrator takes in Dunnet's houses and their
relationship to one another and to the natural landscape remains
throughout the narrative; although not belabored, it shows up
again in her description of Mrs. Todd's house, the schoolhouse,
Mrs. Blackett's house, Joanna's house, the Bowden house, and
Elijah Tilley's house. The principal features of the aesthetic the
narrator extols are simplicity, smallness, tidiness, reserve, prac-
ticality, and cheerfulness.

Except for the Bowden house, to which I will return, all of the
important houses in *The Country of the Pointed Firs* are white, frame,
woman-centered structures that perfectly accommodate themselves to their Maine habitat. In the narrator's descriptions, they
simultaneously blend into their natural environment with their
smallness, woodenness, and clever adaptability to terrain; and
they stand out from it, punctuate it brightly with their whiteness
against the dark pines. The social experience that this architecture
articulates is clear. It is corporate yet respectful of privacy, individ-
uated but not class-structured. As historians of material culture
routinely point out, "Spatial patterns do not just happen, they are
caused." Human landscape operates as an "extension of ideological process."[5]

Such axioms of material-culture study find obvious expression
in *The Country of the Pointed Firs*. The second sentence of the book
concentrates on

> the few houses which seemed to be securely wedged and tree-
> nailed in among the ledges by the Landing. These houses made the
> most of their seaward view, and there was a gayety and determined
> floweriness in their bits of garden ground; the small-paned high
> windows in the peaks of their steep gables were like knowing eyes
> that watched the harbor and the far sea-line beyond, or looked
> northward all along the shore and its background of spruces and
> balsam firs. (p. 1)

Jewett's narrator says late in the narrative that she can "read the
history of Mrs. Tilley's best room from its very beginning" (p. 124).
Here she uses the material landscape to introduce us to the values
of the town. These wedged and tree-nailed houses with their gay
gardens and "knowing eyes" say that the people in this place

realize that life is hard, believe that people should adapt to the rocky land rather than try to force it to obey them, maintain an alert watchfulness, and do so with good cheer – even a dash of gaiety (the gardens). The opening architectural vocabulary of *The Country of the Pointed Firs*, in other words, offers a quite standard reading of place and culture. Small-town New England in Jewett's text is made up of ordinary people's houses expressing ordinary Yankee values of ingenuity, pragmatism, cautiousness, good humor, and visual simplicity.

Mrs. Todd's house, the first we see in any detail, reinforces and then specializes this initial reading by adding to it the first in a series of emphases on houses as women's spaces and on the home as the site of business and therefore the foundation of economic life in the area. Almira Todd supports herself by taking in an occasional lodger, such as the narrator, and by dispensing herbs to people who come to her door. Both of these business activities are home-based, run by a woman, and, apparently, economically viable; although Mrs. Todd is not rich, neither is she poor. But the economic point is even more fundamental than that, for the narrator's rhetoric places exaggerated emphasis on Mrs. Todd's house as a place of business, with the word "business" appearing five times in four paragraphs (pp. 6–7). As with any overdetermined interpretation, this superobvious presence calls attention not only to itself but also to what is absent: in this case, factories, warehouses, stores, other commercial buildings, multiple dwellings, mansions, and slums. These absences imply that in Dunnet there is no division between home life and work life because there is no developed capitalist-based class system with managers (the rich) and workers (the poor) – both of which by the time Jewett wrote *The Country of the Pointed Firs* were standard features not only of city life but also of small-town life. An occasional serving girl receives mention (e.g., p. 96), which signals awareness of some class differences. Nevertheless, the time frame of the book – the historical era Jewett has her narrator see and represent in the 1890s – is distanced and idealized. It is preindustrial, unusually free of corrosive class divisions, and remarkably untouched by violence, crime, or unsightly poverty.

Another significant way in which the text suggests that we have journeyed not simply into another area but into a highly inter-preted representation of another era, of a different historical frame, is through the narrator's representation of Mrs. Todd as a witch. As the breeze comes through "the low end-window of the house laden with not only sweet-brier and sweet mary, but balm and sage and borage and mint, wormwood, and southernwood" (p. 3), Almira works in her garden where

> there were some strange and pungent odors that roused a dim sense and remembrance of something in the forgotten past. Some of these might once have belonged to sacred and mystic rites, and have had some occult knowledge handed with them down the centuries.
> (p. 4)

This rhetoric is designed to reassure us that the past of "sacred and mystic rites" and "occult knowledge" has disappeared. But has it? Why are we told that Mrs. Todd brews compounds in a "small caldron" for neighbors who come "by night as if by stealth, bring-ing their own ancient-looking vials to be filled"? Or that some nostrums, such as the "Indian remedy," come with "whispered directions," and others require "cautions," secrecy, and "muttered long chapters of directions" (p. 4)? The narrator's reading of Mrs. Todd as a witch and therefore of the time she inhabits as one in which witchcraft still lives is repeatedly stressed. Indeed, the narra-tor's last view of Mrs. Todd at the end of this chapter reasserts the witch association, showing the towering woman in her house "in the centre of a braided rug, and its rings of black and gray seemed to circle about her feet in the dim light" (p. 8).[6]

The narrator's attention to Mrs. Todd's material reality reinforces the idea that she is part of a highly interpreted – a heavily "read" – past. It is important that her house is small, modest, and organized around one chimney. In this domestic space outdoors and indoors intermingle, with the garden entering the house in the form of various scents and fragrances and Mrs. Todd moving between house and garden as between two rooms. Establishing harmony between the worlds of nature and domesticity, this indoor/outdoor house also maintains that there is no split between public and private realms. Although her house is Mrs. Todd's personal dwell-ing, it is also a public space – a boardinghouse from time to time and, at all times, a friendly woman-centered variation on the New

England country store. As such it serves as a social center, appropriately located on the edge of town, the place where village and countryside meet, and as a serious place of business. That business, playfully but nevertheless clearly identified as witchcraft, consists of ancient, sacred, mysterious rites best understood and controlled by women and associated more with the seventeenth and eighteenth centuries in New England than with the nineteenth. Finally, Almira's house, we cannot help but notice, contains in its design numerous boundaries and thresholds: fences, gates, windows, and doorways. Each of them, however, appears to allow easy passage. The narrator and Mrs. Todd talk through the window; Mrs. Todd and the doctor converse over the fence; neighbors pass through the gate and up the path, with Mrs. Todd accompanying them back down and out. All of this emphasized materiality creates Mrs. Todd's house as a major text within the text. Although literally located on the edge of town, her house, in the narrator's reading, stands culturally at its center, which she presents as preindustrial and matrifocal, multiple-boundaried yet accessible, and the site of perfectly merged business, domestic, and sacred activities.

It is important to note that this idealized or heavily "read" past in Jewett's text derives from the same physical evidence that professional, modern, material historians study. As Laura Fecych Sprague explains, paraphrasing a more detailed study by Thomas Hubka:

> The most prevalent type of dwelling house in Maine from the mid-eighteenth to the mid-nineteenth century was of one or one-and-one-half stories. One or two rooms deep, the living spaces were built around a central chimney; this arrangement restricted the size of the rooms. To move from one room to another, passage through other rooms was required, thus limiting privacy. This style was frequently found in the countryside.[7]

Jewett's narrator simply takes this basic structure and provides an obviously interpreted version of it, first with Mrs. Todd's house and then with the ones that follow, Mrs. Blackett's, Joanna Todd's, and Elijah Tilley's. The narrator entertains no pretense of noncommittal objectivity or detachment. Although Mrs. Todd's house, with its caldron and circle-casting braid rug, may be the most flamboyantly interpreted, all are places the narrator invests with (from her point of view) positive values. These houses exist for her as spiritual places, virtually shrines.

Holiest is Mrs. Blackett's. Her house stands at the sacred, intimate center of the narrative, where the narrator and Mrs. Todd journey together out to Green Island and then down into the island's mystical, lush plot of pennyroyal, special herb of women.[8] We see at once that this house is special, imbued with high portent, and yet ordinary, typical of the many modest, tidy, tiny domiciles in the area. "A long time before we landed at Green Island we could see the small white house, standing high like a beacon, where Mrs. Todd was born and where her mother lived, on a green slope above the water, with dark spruce woods still higher" (p. 34). The narrator announces her pleasure in the locale of Mrs. Blackett's house, admitting: "One could not help wishing to be a citizen of such a complete and tiny continent and home of fisherfolk" (p. 39). Then she offers us the house itself, outside and in, in highly inflected detail.

The low-walled structure is "broad and clean" with a heavy-looking roof. "It was one of the houses that seem firm-rooted in the ground, as if they were two-thirds below the surface, like icebergs" (p. 39). This grounded house has two entrances: the formal front door with its "orderly vine" on each side and the kitchen entrance with its "mass of gay flowers and greenery, as if they had been swept together by some diligent garden broom in a tangled heap" (p. 39). The narrator is invited to enter through the formal front portal, from which she proceeds to the best room. There the first substantial conversation between mother and daughter takes place, which consists almost entirely of exclamatory compliments, delivered by Mrs. Todd "standing before us like a large figure of Victory" (p. 40), about Mrs. Blackett's having turned the carpet.

All of these details emphasize the importance of material-culture representation in Jewett's book. Various texts are described for us: the exterior of Mrs. Blackett's house, its orientation to the earth, its two entrances, its parlor with newly turned carpet, the scatter rugs over the carpet, the green paper curtains, the room's glass lamps, its "pictures of national interest," and the "crystallized bouquets of grass and some fine shells on the narrow mantelpiece"

(p. 40). Simultaneously, the narrator interprets these things for their social, spiritual, and political functions and meanings. We see how seasonal rituals of renewal merge with social values of conservation and frugality in the turning of the carpet, which is in addition presented as an act of heroic strength for an eighty-six-year-old woman (which it is, of course). We are also informed that the parlor, with its simple organic art objects and patriotic pictures, constitutes a formal ceremonial space for community and family, the space designated for sacramental or state occasions. Mrs. Todd, we learn, was married in this room (p. 40). In these ways we come to see that objects – "things" – do not exist as interesting texture, a nice travel book background for "story," in Jewett's narrative. They *are* story. Read by the narrator for their emotional, spiritual, social, and ethical content, space and objects are indicators of human values, as are rituals, ceremonies, sacraments, and festivals. As the narrator states of Mrs. Blackett's house:

> It was indeed a tribute to Society to find a room set apart for her behests out there on so apparently neighborless and remote an island. Afternoon visits and evening festivals must be few in such a bleak situation at certain seasons of the year, but Mrs. Blackett was one of those who do not live to themselves, and who have long since passed the line that divides mere self-concern from a valued share in whatever Society can give and take. There were those of her neighbors who never had taken the trouble to furnish a best room, but Mrs. Blackett was one who knew the uses of a parlor. (p. 41)

Being one who knows the uses and meanings of rooms, objects, visits, and ceremonies represents a crucial interpretive task throughout *The Country of the Pointed Firs*, first for the narrator and then the reader. By the time we get to Elijah Tilley's house at the end of the book, we know exactly how to read the fact that "the long grass grew close against the high stone step [of his front door], and a snowberry bush leaned over it, top-heavy with the weight of a morning-glory vine that had managed to take what the fishermen might call a half hitch about the door-knob" (pp. 119–20). Similarly, having already been taught how to read Mrs. Todd's and Mrs. Blackett's houses, when we are shown Joanna Todd's tiny reclusive house on Shell-heap Island we know how to inter-

88

pret its meager yet telling materiality: its ultratidiness and the bits of shells on the walls with flowers in them. Much as nuances of etiquette and social behavior serve in the traditional novel of manners to tell the reader how to read, so material culture functions in Jewett's text to guide attention and shape reaction. Tilley's blocked front door, the formal entrance to his house, tells us how isolated he is from familial and communal ceremonial life in Dunnet – even as his dead wife's "glass vases on the mantelpiece with their prim bunches of bleached swamp grass and dusty marsh rosemary" (p. 124) declare his lingering desire not to be hopelessly cut off. So, too, Joanna's spotless housekeeping and decorative shells and blossoms attach her to both the ethic and the aesthetic of the community she has left; she has not totally cut herself off, even if she thinks she has.

My argument so far emphasizes how the narrator's interpretive acts in *The Country of the Pointed Firs* guide ours. She teaches us how to read the material texts she provides; we get the knack and start imitating her; and finally we end up sharing her reading of the country of the pointed firs – namely, that Dunnet is a wonderful, psychically recoverable, "real" part of the American past that we need to go back to, at least periodically or in spirit, to reconnect with the essential mysterious healing values of matrifocal, preindustrial, rustic America. Given this perspective, of course we end by eating a house. We have been celebrating houses as secular shrines throughout the narrative.

The issue I now wish to raise is the problem inherent in any textual interpretation – namely, that the teacher's reading is not the only one possible. Indeed, within *The Country of the Pointed Firs* itself the question of the relationship between authority and interpretation is repeatedly raised. Following Jewett's lead, I want in the second half of this essay to look through the narrator's proferred reading of material culture to the author's text on empire.

Early in the book Jewett invites us to rebel against rote obedience to pedagogic authority and precedent. The narrator, making visible what we already know to be the case because of the book we hold in our hands, announces her intention to be "the teacher." She seats herself authoritatively behind the desk of the

Dunnet schoolhouse – a structure that itself, in its whiteness, framedness, simplicity, airiness, and small scale, at first seems no more than a clever variation on the other sacred female-centered domestic spaces in the book. Once seated, however, the narrator finds herself wrestling with complex issues of authority, knowledge, silence, and speech.

The scene throws into confusion basic Eurocentric assumptions about texts and teachers. First, the schoolhouse is an empty space, one that has no body of learners. Pictured thus in a book that argues the importance of learning about life directly from life, it formally questions what material historians call "the evidential priority of the written word."[9] The hollow building stands for the privileging of written texts that the narrator has to learn to leave behind, at least for the summer. It confirms the necessity of learning to read material life in *The Country of the Pointed Firs*. Second, and equally important, the teaching that does take place in the empty schoolhouse is not the teaching of a woman. One may sit behind the desk, but the figure truly at home in this deserted building is male. Despite her authoritative perch, the narrator finds herself intruded upon by an irksome, then baffling, and finally pitiful old interpreter of strange, dead, distant material texts, an addled old man with a passion for Milton and a head full of ghosts and frightening, violent tales. The apt name of this weird little man in the schoolhouse, this unexpected, deranged teacher, is Littlepage.

Littlepage's text is material – it is a real place he says he has been – yet it is oddly unmaterial. Its cold, freezing contours keep disappearing into the haze; its buildings and inhabitants keep evaporating into shadows. Placed early in Jewett's text about interpreting texts and quite purposefully introduced in the schoolhouse, site of elite Western patriarchal culture's insistence that the most important texts to be read are books, not things, this scene juxtaposes the two very different teachers/interpreters/writers, Littlepage and the narrator: one dominant and the other impotent. He, in an obvious parody of erudite masculine learning gone berserk, offers a hyperbookish interpretation of a material text that does not seem even to exist. She, in an equally parodic textual gesture, sits "at the teacher's desk as if I were that great authority, with all the timid empty benches in rows before me" (p. 12), and finds herself unable to fill the blank pages in front of her.

For a while Littlepage's lecture, although boring at first, succeeds in capturing the narrator's interest. She finds herself drawn into his strange ultramasculine Western way of knowing that, quite appropriately, is preoccupied with interpreting great white male material texts of conquest and danger. He describes ships that are tiny floating isolates of incredibly specialized knowledge and scientific expeditions that travel to the ends of the earth to find great frozen towns beyond the boundaries of human warmth and communication. But finally this type of knowledge is less important than what the narrator can learn outside the schoolhouse: Littlepage's narrative is included early on and then left behind in *The Country of the Pointed Firs*. Indeed, it is probably one of this book's most radical moves to label the great heroic adventures and texts of white men as curious but finally minor – marginal – compared with what really matters in life.[10] In any case, only when the narrator leaves the schoolhouse and Littlepage behind – only when she gets out from behind the desk, rebels against the teacher, and resolves instead to learn from what she sees and hears out of school – does she really put herself in the position of having something to teach.

One of the most important texts the narrator teaches from is the Bowden reunion, the ceremony close to the end of *The Country of the Pointed Firs*. Ritual celebration of family and environment, the question of how to teach, and the whole subject of texts, textual interpretation, and the sacramental feeding of human beings merge in an end-of-the-summer festival literally enacted in space surrounding the old ancestral Bowden house.

The usual way of reading the Bowden reunion – the way the narrator interprets it for us and thus implicitly instructs us to do likewise – is as a naive, joyful, old-fashioned rural festival affirming traditional American values of family loyalty, sainted motherhood, abiding patriotism, and spontaneous benevolent accord with nature. In this view the reunion rejoices in an older, simpler America, one before the advent of factories and skyscrapers, huge cities and automobiles. Even more particularly, many white feminist critics, myself included, have written fondly of this reunion and of the book as a whole as a celebratory mythologization of a rural matrifocal community in which women – Mrs. Todd and Mrs. Blackett – have real power and status, a place outside of or, in historical metaphor, "before" patriarchal hegemony.[11]

Yet if we attend carefully to the presentation of the festival in the text, a quite different, and I think for Jewett lovers disconcerting, interpretation of the reunion is required. In the narrator's reading of the reunion, which we must then see as coloring the whole text, the ritual celebrates not just rural life but specifically the transplantation of Anglo-Norman culture onto North American soil. The reunion celebrates, in a word, the triumphant colonization of Indian land by white people of British and Norman ancestry.[12] What we commemorate when we eat the word(s) and swallow the house is white imperialism.

Traces of empire – tiny trophies from "exotic" foreign ports and colonies – pop up throughout *The Country of the Pointed Firs*. We are told that Mrs. Beggs, married three times to seafaring men, inhabited a house that "was decorated with West Indian curiosities" (p. 13). When they visit her mother, Mrs. Todd shows the narrator the "old flowered-glass tea-caddy" and drinking mugs that her father, she explains, "brought home to my mother from the island of Tobago," a British colony off the coast of Venezuela (p. 51). Upon leaving Dunnet, the narrator receives from Mrs. Todd two precious gifts, a coral pin and a "quaint West Indian basket" (p. 131). When she visits Mrs. Todd, Mrs. Fosdick protests that she doesn't want any tea made out of "none o' your useful herbs"; she wants "some o' that Oolong you keep in the little chist" (p. 57). Later when Mrs. Todd talks about Shell-heap Island, Mrs. Fosdick exclaims: "Ought to see them painted savages I've seen when I was young out in the South Sea Islands!" (p. 64).

Close to home, Shell-heap Island is described in considerable detail by Mrs. Fosdick:

> "'Twas 'counted a great place in old Indian times; you can pick up their stone tools 'most any time if you hunt about. There's a beautiful spring o' water, too. Yes, I remember when they used to tell queer stories about Shell-heap Island. Some said 'twas a great bangeing-place [lounging place] for the Indians, and an old chief resided there once that ruled the winds; and others said they'd always heard that once the Indians come down from up country an'

left a captive there without any bo't, an' 'twas too far to swim across
to Black Island, so called, an' he lived there till he perished."
  "I've heard say he walked the island after that, and sharp-sighted
folks could see him an' lose him like one o' them citizens Cap'n
Littlepage was acquainted with up to the north pole," announced
Mrs. Todd grimly. "Anyway, there was Indians – you can see their
shell-heap that named the island; and I've heard myself that 'twas
one o' their cannibal places, but I never could believe it. There never
was no cannibals on the coast o' Maine. All the Indians o' these
regions are tame-looking folks." (p. 63)

Although the reading here is meant to be friendly – Indians Mrs.
Todd knows of are "tame-looking" – the racism and ethnocentri-
cism of this quick sketch are inescapable. Mrs. Todd's "queer stories" deal in familiar white stereotypes of Indians: they are lazy
("bangeing"), cruel (the abandoned captive), slippery (the comparison to Littlepage's disappearing wraiths), and uncivilized (the
cannibal theory). Everything in the description points to the foreignness, the strangeness of Indians, to their differences from Dunnet folk, about whom the question of looking "tame" or not does
not even arise. Further, the association of Indians with the most
deviant and maladjusted of Dunneters, Joanna, is hardly acciden-
tal. Naturally she goes to live on the same island they liked; it just
shows how far outside the circle of ideal white community she has
perversely pitched herself.

The function of all this colonial exotica – whether tea caddies
from the other side of the equator or shells left on an island from
pre-Dunnet days – is to situate Dunnet at the center of a far-flung
empire. It does not matter that the town's seafaring heyday has
passed; Dunnet still occupies a position of cultural power. Colonial
artifacts in *The Country of the Pointed Firs* inscribe on an otherwise
homogeneous material landscape the presence of obvious racial
and ethnic differences that are successfully contained and therefore controlled by being totally surrounded by – taken into and
reduced to minority status within – the dominant culture, which
celebrates and affirms its white roots each year at the Bowden
reunion.

Quite accurately, the narrator reads the reunion as a political
and spiritual event of major importance in the local culture. As
Robert Blair St. George points out, festivals should always be read

as constructed cultural landscapes. People create and use specific "ritual space in order to reveal to themselves periodically the inner structure of their own lives."[13] In addition, as John Brooke emphasizes in a discussion of death and burial customs in early New England, collective ritual practice frequently enables a group to deal with "threats of disharmony and disunion" by creating "structurally and symbolically powerful events" that bring individuals and households together. As we see in Jewett's narrative, the purpose of such rituals, "requiring the mobilization of formal religious categories, the manipulation of material symbols, and the binding of the community to the province's mythic past,"[14] is to strengthen the participants by affirming the values that unite them.

The values that unite the Bowden revelers are communicated in the language and metaphors the narrator uses to describe the ritual. Most obvious is her pattern of regal and feudal rhetoric and imagery. Seated "with much majesty" (p. 90) in the front of the wagon, Mrs. Todd undertakes a royal progress with her mother and the narrator to get to the reunion; they wave and occasionally even descend to converse with people as they wend their ceremonial way. Once at the reunion, Mrs. Todd announces with pride: "Mother's always the queen," at which point the old woman is duly "escorted" to the house where she holds "court" (pp. 98, 99). Meanwhile Mrs. Todd receives "her own full share of honor" from men whose kindness "was the soul of chivalry" (pp. 98–9).

The antiquity and sacredness of this Bowden aristocracy find reinforcement in numerous classical references throughout the book, such as the well-known comparison of Mrs. Todd to Antigone (p. 49) and the narrator's specific statement that those at the reunion "might have been a company of ancient Greeks going to celebrate a victory, or to worship the god of harvests" (p. 100). But as Sandra Zagarell has argued,[15] the ancientness of the royal line of Bowdens also receives distinctly northern European definition. Evoking vague notions of prehistoric blood ties and ancient scattered ritual fires on dark heaths, the narrator opines:

> When, at long intervals, the altars to patriotism, to friendship, to the ties of kindred, are reared in our familiar fields, then the fires glow, the flames come up as if from the inexhaustible burning heart of the earth; the primal fires break through the granite dust in which our

souls are set. Each heart is warm and every face shines with the
ancient light. (p. 96)

Recalling the witch imagery earlier in the book, this evocation of
primal fires and ancient altars reared in familiar fields calls up a
dim European past that the narrator goes on to name. First she
says: "We were no more a New England family celebrating its own
existence and simple progress; we carried the tokens and inheritance of all such households from which this had descended, and
were only the latest of our line. We possessed the instincts of a far,
forgotten childhood; I found myself thinking that we ought to be
carrying green branches and singing as we went" (p. 100). Then
she specifically identifies the particular "line" of these people as
Anglo-Norman. She calls attention to "the curiously French type
of face which prevailed in this rustic company," points out that
"Mrs. Blackett was plainly of French descent," and observes that
"a large proportion of the early settlers on this northern coast of
New England were of Huguenot blood" because "it is the Norman
Englishman, not the Saxon, who goes adventuring to a new
world" (pp. 102–3). She later gazes on the assembled company
and thinks: "So . . . their ancestors may have sat in the great hall
of some old French house in the Middle Ages" (p. 105).

Most telling, however, is the military and religious rhetoric that
surrounds the regal imagery and the references to ancient Anglo-
Norman lines and lore. These representations declare that the ritual behavior enacted by Jewett's New World Anglo-Normans consists of marching like an army and then worshiping as a body the
supreme material artifact in the book: the original, ancestral, Bowden house, which is, ultimately, sacramentally consumed in the
form of cake.

The military imagery is blatant. As soon as the reunioners gather, there emerges from the group a "straight, soldierly little figure
of a man" who bears an uncanny resemblance to Mrs. Blackett
and who proceeds to "marshall" the crowd into ranks. He has a
"grand military sort of courtesy" and everyone obeys him. The
company stands "as speechless as a troop to await his order. Even
the children were ready to march" (p. 99). Upon Mrs. Blackett and
the ministers' taking their place at the head, this small army of

Anglo-Normans marches off in orderly formation. Their "long procession," described as one of the ancient human "rites" witnessed by sky and sea through the centuries, ends in a grove that forms a natural cathedral. There the "great family," momentarily looking small in the huge outdoor nave, congregates beneath "a thick growth of dark pines and firs with an occasional maple or oak that gave a gleam of color like a bright window in the great roof." On three sides of this outdoor church, water is visible through the tree trunks. But on the fourth "we could see the green sunlit field we had just crossed as if we looked out at it from a dark room, and the old house and its lilacs standing placidly in the sun" (p. 100).

Framed on the altar-wall of their outdoor cathedral, the Bowden ancestral house forms the focal point for worship in this sylvan sanctuary where the large family originally from Europe comes each year to rest and rejoice. In this space the narrator observes how French everyone looks (p. 101), and then immediately there arises the issue of foreigners – who is in and who is out of this lineage. One reunioner, to emphasize the foreignness of one person, remarks with easy racism: "I always did think Mari' Harris resembled a Chinee" (p. 103). Then the merry white people proceed to their long, orderly feast tables, where, ending the ritual, Mrs. Todd and the narrator eat the words "Bowden" and "Reunion" and a large number of reunioners partake of the gingerbread replica of the Bowden house, which is shared "not without seriousness, and as if it were a pledge and token of loyalty" (p. 108).

The Bowden reunion is about racial purity and white cultural dominance. It celebrates white ethnic pride, the extended Bowden family's Anglo-Norman lineage, which is militantly asserted and religiously affirmed in all the orderly marching and solemn worshiping. In earlier discussions of *The Country of the Pointed Firs* I have held that the most intense part of the book, its dramatic climax, occurs at its center, in Chapters 8 through 11, when the narrator and Mrs. Todd bond in the dense field of pennyroyal on Green Island. I have argued against interpreting the Bowden reunion chapters as the book's culmination. But now I have to ask how much my argument has reflected Jewett's design, which I do think is there, and how much it has been the result of my resisting another design, which is also there: the subtle but clear protofacist implications of all those white people marching around in military formation ritualistically affirming their racial purity, global dominance, and white ethnic superiority and solidarity.

There is no escaping that the communion at the end of *The Country of the Pointed Firs* is about colonialism. When we eat the words and swallow the house, what we take into ourselves according to the terms of the collective ritual the narrator has just finished so carefully interpreting for us are the signifiers of the Anglo-Norman conquest of North America. Karen Oakes points out that it would have been impossible for Jewett, writing in the 1880s and 1890s, to be ignorant of dominant-culture theories of racial purity and white superiority in late-nineteenth-century America and then offers the interesting thought that we might read Mrs. Todd as

> a person whose heritage is (at least metaphorically) mixed-blood; for she possesses the herbal skill not only of her colonial counterparts but of her Indian predecessors. Furthermore, we learn in another story, "The Foreigner," that Mrs. Todd has acquired much of her insight from a woman who parallels the figure of the Indian outsider, a French woman from Jamaica, who significantly cannot speak "Maine" and horrifies her sober and asexual counterparts by singing and dancing in the meetinghouse vestry in a shockingly "natural" manner.[16]

But we also have to ask: What does it mean to be "metaphorically mixed-blood" in a text so heavily inscribed with the glories, privileges, and purity of the white race except that Mrs. Todd is intelligent enough to respect the wisdom of the indigenous people who were there before her? That is something – respect for people whose lifeways differ from one's own. But it is not all that much. The fact is that Dunnet as represented in Jewett's text is built on the ruins of American Indian civilization (no live Indians appear in the book), and it is decorated by the trophies of empire: baskets from the Caribbean, tea from China, mugs from South America. All those tiny, tidy, white, fenced, tree-nailed, and wedged houses staring up and down the coast do articulate a vision of preindustrial matrifocal harmony, health, and happiness. But they also stand for white colonial settlement and dominance. When we take communion with Mrs. Todd and the narrator, we are swallowing not just the former but also the latter.

NOTES

1. Sarah Orne Jewett, *The Country of the Pointed Firs* (1896), ed. Mary Ellen Chase, intro. Marjorie Pryse (New York: Norton, 1982); page numbers cited in the text refer to this edition.

2. For detailed discussions see Elizabeth Ammons, *Conflicting Stories: American Women Writers at the Turn into the Twentieth Century* (New York: Oxford Univ. Press, 1991), chap. 4, which revises and expands my earlier discussion, "Going in Circles: The Female Geography of Jewett's *Country of the Pointed Firs,*" *Studies in the Literary Imagination* 16 (1983): 83–92.

3. Robert Blair St. George, ed., *Material Life in America, 1600–1860* (Boston: Northeastern Univ. Press, 1988), p. 3.

4. Ibid., p. 8.

5. Ibid., pp. 371, 357.

6. I discuss this imagery, as well as witch imagery in other Jewett fiction, in "Jewett's Witches," in Gwen L. Nagel, ed., *Critical Essays on Sarah Orne Jewett* (Boston: Hall, 1984), pp. 165–84.

7. Laura Fecych Sprague, ed., *Agreeable Situations: Society, Commerce, and Art in Southern Maine, 1780–1830* (Kennebunk, Me.: Brick Store Museum; distributed by Northeastern University Press, 1987), p. 107. The study Sprague cites is Thomas Hubka, *Big House, Little House, Back House, Barn* (Hanover, N.H.: Univ. Press of New England, 1984).

8. A detailed discussion of this scene and of the relationship between the narrator and Mrs. Todd can be found in Ammons, *Conflicting Stories.*

9. St. George, ed., *Material Life,* p. 8.

10. For a stimulating discussion of various ways in which Jewett exploits the category of "minor" and turns it to her advantage in an earlier piece of fiction, see Louis A. Renza, *"A White Heron" and the Question of Minor Literature* (Madison: Univ. of Wisconsin Press, 1984).

11. For a cross section of such white feminist readings, see Ammons, *Conflicting Stories;* Josephine Donovan, *Sarah Orne Jewett* (New York: Ungar, 1980) and *After the Fall: The Demeter–Persephone Myth in Wharton, Cather, and Glasgow* (University Park, Pa.: Penn State Univ. Press, 1989); Marcia McClintock Folsom, "'Tact Is a Kind of Mind-Reading': Empathic Style in Sarah Orne Jewett's *The Country of the Pointed Firs,*" in Nagel, ed., *Critical Essays,* pp. 76–88; Karen Oakes, "'All That Lay Deepest in Her Heart': Reflections on Jewett, Gender, and Genre," *Colby Quarterly* 26 (1990): 152–60; Marjorie Pryse, "Introduction to the Norton Edition," in *The Country of the Pointed Firs,* ed. Chase, pp. v–xix; Sarah Way Sherman, *Sarah Orne Jewett, an*

American Persephone (Hanover, N.H.: Univ. Press of New England, 1989); Sandra Zagarell, "Narrative of Community: The Identification of a Genre," *Signs* 13 (1988): 498–527. A recent, excellent book from an African-American feminist perspective is Marilyn Sanders Mobley, *Folk Roots and Mythic Wings in Sarah Orne Jewett and Toni Morrison: The Cultural Function of Narrative* (Baton Rouge: Louisiana State Univ. Press, 1991).

12. For my initial recognition of the importance of race and imperialism in *The Country of the Pointed Firs* I am greatly indebted to Sandra Zagarell's paper, "Homogeneity and Difference: The Narratives of Community of Sarah Orne Jewett and Alice Dunbar-Nelson," delivered at the Modern Language Association Convention, Chicago, December 1990, and developed and expanded in her discussion in this volume (see Chapter 2). Also very influential have been Karen Oakes's remarks, and particularly her references to Paula Gunn Allen's work, in "'All That Lay Deepest.'"

13. St. George, ed., *Material Life*, pp. 10, 12.

14. John L. Brooke, "'For Honour and Civil Worship to Any Worthy Person': Burial, Baptism, and Community on the Massachusetts Near Frontier, 1730–1790," St. George, ed., *Material Life in America*, p. 464.

15. See note 12.

16. Oakes, "'All That Lay Deepest,'" pp. 157–8. For an extended, excellent discussion of the racist ideological context in which most middle-class white women wrote in the United States at the turn into the twentieth century, see Susan S. Lanser, "Feminist Criticism, 'The Yellow Wallpaper,' and the Politics of Color in America," *Feminist Studies* 15 (1989): 415–41. Also, I discuss ideologies of race, the effects of racism, and the work of turn-of-the-century women writers at length in *Conflicting Stories.*

5

Regionalism and Nationalism
in Jewett's *Country*
of the Pointed Firs

SUSAN GILLMAN

IN most American literary histories, the late-nineteenth-century turn in fiction toward region is assumed to signal a rejection of nation and national issues. Regionalism is envisioned as a limited form, just as "local color" is seen, sometimes pejoratively, more recently affirmatively, as a minor literature associated with local places, "little" forms, and women. Regions as various as Jewett's New England, the pre–Civil War South of George Washington Cable, Thomas Dixon, and others, and the quasi-mythic, Roman or medieval settings of popular historical romances are treated as though they inhabit Jackson Lears's "no place of grace."[1] That is, such constructed regions are thought of as symptomatic of the flight from modernism and the sense of placelessness that Lears sees as endemic to turn-of-the-century U.S. culture. If not exactly party to Lears's "antimodernist impulse," these constructions are grouped together under the banner of nostalgia, as backward glances at supposedly simpler, more cohesive ways of life characteristic of pre–Civil War America.

As a critical lens, regionalism thus implicitly "Americanizes" these regions, turning *Ben Hur*'s Rome and Jewett's Dunnet Landing alike into embodiments of a prelapsarian, utopian "America." Regionalism homogenizes its imagined regions even as it excludes historical change as an active participant in the production of regional writing. The only "history" generally associated with regionalists is static, containing categories of literary history or such set pieces of monumental history as the decline of rural life under industrialism. Otherwise, it is thought, regionalists respond to national conflict – whether over old sectional and racial divisions or new ethnic and economic tensions – by turning their backs on it.

101

I want to suggest, however, that there is a significant link between regionalism and nationalism, one that includes but goes beyond simple rejection. All of the very different novels under the regionalist umbrella share the powerful memory of the Civil War, paradoxically enacting, as Amy Kaplan puts it, "a willed amnesia about founding conflicts, while they reinvent multiple and contested pasts to claim as the shared origin of national identity."[2] Within the Sarah Orne Jewett mini-industry, however, the Civil War is rarely mentioned. Nor is the postbellum cultural project of national reunification that so occupied the United States in the last two decades of the nineteenth century, when Jewett was well into her writing career. That project imprinted itself on the American landscape in a range of political and cultural phenomena: in the legal underwriting of segregation at both the state and federal court levels; in such public reminiscing about the war itself as the *Century* magazine series "Battles and Leaders of the Civil War" (which included patriotic pieces by Confederate and Union soldiers, as well as Twain's satiric "Private History of a Campaign That Failed"); and, perhaps most relevant to Jewett, in the widespread vogue for southern "local color," with its nostalgia for the lost cause that reunited the sections of the country by rewriting the past, culminating in 1915 with D. W. Griffith's version of a new American history, *The Birth of a Nation.*

Rather than placing Jewett in this historical context, however, critical debates focus on her "place" in the canon and are dominated by the same aesthetic and formal questions. Is Jewett a regionalist or a realist? Is the apparently plotless *Country of the Pointed Firs* a novel, or does it have a different kind of structure? The same critical passages continue to be quoted again and again. Most often cited is Willa Cather's statement that *Country* is one of three American books – *Scarlet Letter* and *Huck Finn* are the others – with "the possibility of a long, long life. . . . I can think of no others that confront time and change so serenely. . . . A masterpiece! . . . a message in a universal language. . . ."[3] This kind of formalist response applies both to the critics of the "impoverished" literature of "New England in decline" in the 1930s and 1940s (Parrington, Brooks) and, perhaps more surprisingly, to recent feminist work, which celebrates Jewett's work by resituating it

102

within "women's culture," "a woman's tradition" (of New England local-color literature), and "female geography."[4] Though clearly an important corrective to an earlier, unacknowledged masculinist bias, this effort has tended to construct an essentialized rather than historicized conception of woman, the criticism oddly reproducing the "escape from the masculine time of history into transcending feminine space" attributed to *Country* itself. Though coming to different assessments of Jewett's place and value, all of these critical projects recapitulate her exclusion from history. In short, it appears that the Jewett critic, like "a lover of Dunnet Landing," may return even today to the Jewett landscape "to find the unchanged shores of the pointed firs."[5]

What difference might it make to read Jewett, whom, after all, no one would claim rightfully belongs in Edmund Wilson's *Patriotic Gore*, in the context of national conflict and reunion? This is not simply a matter of Jewett's having occasionally entered what Albion Tourgée called "The South as a Field for Fiction" (1888), in the form of several southern local-color stories and many references to the Civil War in *Country* and other stories. Nor is it only an issue of the racialized thinking that Jewett displayed in her lifelong concern with ancestors and lineage. Nor is it even the raw association Jewett herself made between the war and her own personal and cultural losses: "My grandfather died in my eleventh year, and presently the Civil War began. From that time the simple village life was at an end."[6]

Much more significant are the ways that *Country*'s confrontation with a "New England in decline" negotiates problems of past and present loss and thus speaks to the cultural reconciliation process under way twenty years after the national losses of the Civil War. Both efforts center on conflicts over reinterpretation of the past and its relation to the present. As what Eric Sundquist calls a "literature of memory," Jewett's local-color participates in the double-edged nostalgia characteristic of so much American literature of this period, devoted to enshrining the Civil War and the history of slavery in order to defuse their fratricidal energies and underwrite a new era of national reunion – and of new racial and ethnic divisions.[7] How, then, does Jewett's shifting representation, sometimes elegiac, sometimes celebratory, of the heroic (some would say, male) past and the domesticated (female) present locate her in a particular gendered place on what has been called the "road to reunion"?[8]

The national project of reunion reinterpreted, and often re-created, the past in contradictory ways: as preindustrial, plantation idyll whose demise either implicitly or explicitly initiates present racial violence (Thomas Nelson Page, George Washington Cable, Thomas Dixon) or as locus of racial and sexual violence that continues, implicitly or explicitly, into the present (Mark Twain, Pauline Hopkins, Frances Harper). For Jewett's characters and readers, the conflict in *Country* centers on differing interpretations of the past in both time and space. The debate over Dunnet Landing as fallen from a time of former, commercial glory or preserving the simplicities of a mythic past, "the instincts of a far, forgotten childhood," parallels the question of whether the town, as a rural space, is a therapeutic or stultifying retreat from the urban. Gender complicates these questions, with the chronological-fall narrative associated predominantly with the male viewpoint and the spatial paradise associated with the female. To some, notably Captain Littlepage, speaking for the once-glorious life at sea that made "men of those who followed it," "shipping's a terrible loss to this part o' New England from a social point o' view;" to others, most explicitly the narrator, the decline of shipping accounts merely for the "sad disappearance of sea-captains," since Dunnet Landing as a whole remains a place of timeless ritual, mostly but by no means all female in nature (p. 20).

The vexed chronological relation of past to present that at times divides the town's lonely former sea captains from its neighborly women thriving on a combination of social and natural rhythms is further complicated when that relation is spatialized. First, the conflict over female and male conceptions of time is superimposed on the urban versus rural axis associated with the narrator, who continually contrasts the virtues of village life – its mixture of remoteness, quaintness, and elaborate social conventionalities – with the unspecified rigors of the urban world she has temporarily left behind. Second, the question of time passing or time eternal is extended from the city–country locus that structures much of

Country onto the larger sectional–national front invoked in the long Bowden reunion episode.

In what is sometimes seen as the book's climax, the Bowden family reunion explicitly and for the first time locates Dunnet Landing in the context both of the "New England nature" and of the "great national anniversaries which our country has lately kept" (pp. 95–6, 110). Here, in the context of a yearly ritual, the novel ritualistically returns to, but does not resolve, virtually all of its central conflicts: isolation versus community, exclusion versus inclusion, and, perhaps most important, the shifting degrees of freedom and constraint in men's and women's life experiences of the past and the present. The reunion chapters ("The Bowden Reunion," "The Feast's End") actually concluded *Country* when it first appeared in the *Atlantic Monthly* in serial form in 1896. (Jewett did not add the final two chapters, "Along Shore" and "The Backward View," until the novel was published in book form later that year.) How one reads the reunion episode, either as the climax of a linear narrative or as repetition within a cyclical structure, has become a kind of critical litmus test in Jewett studies, indicating where one stands on the gender spectrum.

Once assumed to be at the very center of *Country*'s narrative of decline, the reunion, with its ancestor worship and sham militarism, has been seen as the culmination of *Country*'s lament for a lost world of international travel and heroism, or what Warner Berthoff describes as "that reference to the life of male action and encounter without which the narrator's sympathy for backwater Dunnet would seem myopic, sentimental." This view has been challenged by feminist readings, such as Elizabeth Ammons's, that instead take the visit to Green Island, the "sacred female space" where the quintessential matriarch Mrs. Blackett lives, as the center, not climactic but "concentric," of the book's celebration of the female world of love and ritual.[9]

The critical dispute over the significance and meaning of the reunion points to the ways that the novel is structured, not around harmony or transcendence but conflict. There is, of course, the question of the narrator's own conflicted relation to Dunnet Landing: on the one hand, her struggle to move from outsider to "near to feeling like a true Bowden," as she says she finally does at the

105

reunion, and, on the other, the conflict between her urbanized view of the village – as a retreat, mythic and timeless, but also ancient and somehow cramped – and the very different perspective of its inhabitants. Most readings of the narrator, whether explicitly feminist or not, acknowledge this double-edged quality, what Amy Kaplan identifies as regionalism's "Janus-faced nostalgia."[10] Yet the townspeople do not represent a homogeneous body of insiders, or even one divided simply along gender lines, but rather struggle over precisely the same issues as the narrator and the critics, conducting what amounts to an open-ended argument running throughout the novel about social structure and gender relations, past and present.

Captain Littlepage is usually remembered as *the* spokes*man* for the once exotic world of men at sea – "it made men of those who followed it" – and against the present confines of life at home, or what the narrator broadly refers to as "the subject of the decadence of shipping interests in all its affecting branches" (pp. 20, 28). But to equate the world of shipping simply with a lost male paradise is to focus on only one part of the captain's retrospective vision, which encompasses the domestic as well as the heroic. In commentary that is not discussed as often as his enigmatic tale of a shipwrecked expedition, he tells the narrator:

> "In the old days, a good part o' the best men here knew a hundred ports and something of the way folks lived in them. They saw the world for themselves, and like's not their wives and children saw it with them. . . . Yes, they lived more dignified, and their houses were better within an' without. Shipping's a terrible loss to this part o' New England from a social point of view, ma'am." (p. 20)

It is the narrator, not Littlepage, who interprets the social loss as predominantly a male one: "It accounts for the change in a great many things," she says, yet names only one, " – the sad disappearance of sea-captains, – doesn't it?" For the captain, the lost beneficiaries of sea travel were not just the men but, more generally, "folks," the lost benefits not just the leaving but the coming home:

> "When folks left home in the old days they left it to some purpose, and when they got home they stayed there and had some pride in it.

There's no large-minded way of thinking now: the worst have got to be best and rule everything; we're all turned upside down and going back year by year." (p. 21)

Littlepage may be adding to the contested narrative of a New England in decline, for so many readers a literary critical fiction that has wrongfully confined Jewett herself, but it is a narrative with more versions than most have acknowledged. He laments not simply an economic but a "social" loss, alluding not merely to a once-simple world of quaint village lifeways but also to a once-wider worldview, shared by both men and women and informed by the cosmopolitanism of travel. Material remnants of those wide horizons linger on in Dunnet Landing's "best things," to use Mrs. Blackett's phrase, the foreign exotica such as "West Indian curiosities," the coral pin Nathan Todd brought "from a port . . . somewheres up the Mediterranean" for "poor Joanna," and other "outlandish things," all fruits of the international trade (pp. 51, 13, 70). The narrator captures the complexly gendered nature of this cosmopolitan vision when she sees in an old daguerreotype of Mrs. Blackett as a girl "a far-off look that sought the horizon; one often sees it in sea-faring families, inherited by girls and boys alike from men who spend their lives at sea" (p. 48).

Captain Littlepage is, then, not the only one who constructs an image of the past as less confining than the present, a time when the freedom and "variety" (a Jewett code word, as we will see) of travel widened the lives of many villagers, at sea and at home alike. Yet this interpretation – for it is that – is contested even within his own terms. At the end of his tale, the captain recalls the occasion for its telling, the funeral of Mrs. Begg, whose loss makes him revert once again to his great theme. "Yes, Mrs. Begg will be very much missed. She was a capital manager for her husband when he was at sea. Oh, yes, shipping is a very great loss" (p. 28). The little we know of the "very much respected Mrs. Begg" both affirms and undercuts Littlepage's ode to the woman keeping the home fires burning. Though she, too, expresses the "great dissatisfaction with town life" characteristic of the male sea captains, rather than look to the sea for relief as they do, she, who "had lived to lament three seafaring husbands," "couldn't get used to [its] constant sound" (p. 13). Captain Littlepage's story of Mrs.

Begg's funeral gives us a subtle version of the narrative of the decline of shipping, in which she plays both a masculine role (once a capital manager, she finds town life as disappointing as any former sea captain) and a feminine role (both her managerial skills and their demise are mediated through three husbands and three widowhoods).

In yet another complexly gendered version of the narrative of decline, we are given Mrs. Todd's old friend, Mrs. Fosdick, "good traveler," "entertaining pilgrim," and mother of a large seafaring family ("sailors and sailors' wives"), most of whom had died before her (p. 59). She speaks much the same line as and, indeed, tells more, perhaps even stranger, tales than Littlepage, though notably without his angst. Having spent part of her life at sea ("like many of the elder women of that coast"), she strikes the narrator as someone whom "in a wider sphere . . . might have [been] called a woman of the world" (p. 59). Her first tale is a striking autobiographical narrative of freedom and transvestism. As an eight-year-old she accompanied her family (including her mother, whose new baby was born "just in time") on a trading voyage bound for the East Indies and, thanks to what appears to be the mother's understandable error in forgetting to take her daughter's clothes, is forced (or privileged, for that is her view) to wear her brother's clothing for "quite a spell of freedom." When her mother finally made her a new skirt, Mrs. Fosdick reports, she was "real discouraged, feeling the hem at my heels every minute, and as if youth were past and gone." The moral of this story of feeling free and then hemmed in once again: "I liked the trousers best; I used to climb the riggin' with 'em and frighten mother till she said an' vowed she'd never take me to sea again" (p. 61).

Mrs. Fosdick clearly goes much farther than Captain Littlepage in celebrating sea travel for its freeing of otherwise rigid gender boundaries, if not for the outright role reversal that Jewett explored, often comically, in a number of stories written during the early 1880s.[11] But in a move characteristic of Jewett's focus on conflicting views among the villagers themselves, Mrs. Todd questions her old friend Mrs. Fosdick's halcyon view of the "old whalin' days," particularly on the woman question. "Whalin' must have been dull for a lady, hardly ever makin' a lively port," asserts Mrs. Todd. "I never desired to go a whalin' v'y'ge myself" (p. 64). Mrs. Fosdick admits to returning to shore feeling behind the times but stresses that it was the "variety" of the traveling life that most attracted her, a Jewett term referring positively to the incorporation of the exotic and the strange *at home*. When "seafarin' families" dominated Dunnet Landing, there were also "a lot o' queer folks" about, whereas, Mrs. Fosdick complains, "everybody's just like everybody else, now" (p. 64). Mrs. Todd understands immediately, having herself already confided to the narrator on the trip to Green Island that "I must say I like variety myself," and accepts the implicit connection her friend assumes between travel at sea and tolerance of difference at home. For both women, as for Captain Littlepage, this relation is formulated as a conflict between past and present, age and youth. "Yes, . . . there was certain a good many curiosities of human natur' in this neighborhood years ago. . . . In these days the young folks is all copy-cats, 'fraid to death they won't be all just alike; as for the old folks, they pray for the advantage o' bein' a little different" (p. 64).

However much the characters might differ on the question of gender relations in the past, everyone agrees that as a community Dunnet Landing has become "narrowed down" (Littlepage's word) in contrast to the wide horizons of the past. Nowhere is the intolerance of difference more apparent than in the disapproval with which Dunnet Landing's two feminized men, William Blackett and Elijah Tilley, are regarded. Mrs. Todd "evidently" thought her brother William a "failure in life" for living, like an unmarried daughter, at home with their mother, to whom he is "son an' daughter both" (pp. 48, 41). "He ought to have made something o' himself, bein' a man an' so like mother," says his more worldly sister (p. 47). A reflection perhaps as much of his being juvenilized as of being feminized, she finds him to have been "always odd," yet it is apparently not the positive sort of "queerness" or "strangeness" that both she and Mrs. Fosdick so admire in their vision of the past (pp. 41, 64). The narrator notes twice that though she can think of "peculiarities of character in the region of Dunnet Landing yet," neither women names any of these contemporary examples (p. 64).

One of those they don't consider might well be Elijah Tilley, the mournful old fisherman, who has become, since his wife's death, as expert at "knittn" as he is at "nettin" and who has made both his house and himself ("a very good housekeeper") into a shrine to her memory (pp. 126, 120). Though he sounds strikingly like one of Mrs. Fosdick's "strange creatures" "that used to hive away in their own houses with some strange notion," he, like William, apparently does not fit the bill. Far from embodying the "energy" Mrs. Todd attributes to the "strangeness" of the past, Tilley knits to pass the moments of "his continual loneliness" (p. 122). Though both William and Elijah exemplify a kind of gender reversal or duality, something like that envisioned in Mrs. Fosdick's transvestite tale, they are not the kind of "queer folks" celebrated in her vision of the past. Rather, their pathetic lives suggest that such gender reversal, and the freedom imagined along with it, are disturbing in the context of present social and economic conditions in Dunnet Landing.

Similarly, we will see, the presence of the foreign in present-day Dunnet Landing is no longer positively cast as "variety," but rather represented as threatening and invasive – unless, that is, the foreign has been reduced to the status of "best things" displayed in "best room" cabinets, remnants of the international trade of the past. Thus we hear a string of exotic place names – Tobago, the East and West Indies, Bordeaux – all associated with the "outlandish things" (p. 28) brought home long ago from sea, but now dissociated from any substantive, living sense of their origins. The predominantly local culture of Dunnet Landing is interlaced with largely unassimilated fragments of both this cosmopolitanism and a nativist popular culture, in the form of various, apparently adventitious references to the Civil War. Brother William sings "the best that lived from the ballad music of the war;" the man who jilted poor Joanna "went to war in one o' the early regiments" and was never heard from again; two feuding farmers who share the same remote island are so estranged, Mrs. Todd says, that "when the news come that the war was over, one of 'em knew it a week, and never stepped across his wall to tell the other" (pp. 53, 78, 34). And, of course, there is the omnipresent absence of young men in Dunnet Landing, among them Bowdens who are not even buried in the family burial ground, "some lost at sea, and some out West, and some who died in the war" (pp. 97–8). Fragmentary pieces of the war, like the shipping industry, seem to be everywhere yet nowhere in Dunnet Landing.

The Bowden reunion brings all of these conflicts to a head, partly by putting them in a broad, national context, partly by explicitly naming them in a broadly recognizable cultural vocabulary. "An American pie is far to be preferred to its humble ancestor, the English tart," remarks the narrator of the pastry culminating the reunion feast (p. 108). Extending the concern with both nationalism and ancestry, the narrator later frames the reunion in explicit terms of blood, clannishness, and inheritance:

> Perhaps it is the great national anniversaries which our country has lately kept, and the soldiers' meetings that take place everywhere, which have made reunions of every sort the fashion. . . . I fancied that old feuds had been overlooked, and the old saying that blood is thicker than water had again proved itself true, though from the variety of names one argued a certain adulteration of the Bowden traits and belongings. Clannishness is an instinct of the heart, – it is more than a birthright, or a custom; and lesser rights were forgotten in the claim to a common inheritance. (p. 110)

This important passage, along with many others in the Bowden reunion chapters, draws on the popular language blending eugenics and evolution that characterized a wide range of efforts to conceptualize "race" and nation (often viewed as interchangeable) in the late nineteenth century, from scientific racism to W. E. B. Du Bois's lifelong project to reconstruct a global history of the black race.

In the reunion episode Jewett works simultaneously in a number of these conflicting spheres. As Sandra Zagarell argues in Chapter 2 of this volume, there is a recognizably nativist, anti-immigrant note in the conversation of one of the Bowden women: "Somebody observed once that you could pick out the likeness of 'most every sort of a foreigner . . . in our parish. . . . I always did think Mari' Harris resembled a Chinee" (p. 103).[12] In a variant of this exclusionary rhetoric, perhaps growing out of Jewett's own botanical metaphors, she sometimes uses biological terms to char-

111

acterize the Bowden clan. Santin Bowden, the "soldierly little figure" who leads the Bowden family to dinner like a military procession, was rejected for service in the Civil War ("he ain't a sound man, an' they wouldn't have him") but, nevertheless, is described as coming of "soldier stock" (p. 101). The Bowden family was said to have come of "very high folks in France" from whom, Mrs. Todd explains, Santin got his "ability." "'Tain't nothin' he's ever acquired; 'twas born in him" (p. 102). The narrator also speaks on behalf of biology and heredity when struck by the "curiously French type of face" among the Bowdens, which she attributes to the "Huguenot blood" of a large proportion of the early settlers of the northern New England coast (pp. 101–2).

But at this point the narrator appeals to the notion of the "gifts" of a particular familial, that is to say, national, heritage. Starting with Mrs. Blackett, "plainly of French descent, in both her appearance and charming gifts," the narrator muses, "I began to respect the Bowdens for their inheritance of . . . a certain pleasing gift of formality" (pp. 101, 105). This approach to ancestry signals an important Jewett swerve away from a biological to a cultural conception of nation and race. One of the best-known nineteenth-century spokesmen for this view, Du Bois argued in "The Conservation of Races" (1897) that each nation, like each "race group," is "striving, each in its own way, to develop for civilization its particular message, its particular ideal."[13] He might also have said its particular gifts, as in the gifts that the black race has "given America, its only American music, its only American fairy tales" (p. 81). Even Du Bois's evolutionary narrative of race development from a semimythologized African childhood onward – "we are Negroes, members of a vast historic race that from the very dawn of creation has slept, but half awakening in the dark forests of its African fatherland (p. 81)" – has its counterpart in the mythic Greek past Jewett's narrator imagines for the Bowdens. "We might have been a company of ancient Greeks going to celebrate a victory," she says of the Bowden family procession.

> We were no more a New England family celebrating its own existence and simple progress; we carried the tokens and inheritance of all such households from which this had descended, and were only

112

the latest of our line. We possessed the instincts of a far, forgotten childhood. (100)

Not only does Jewett construct her own evolutionary narrative for the Bowdens, but she also militarizes the family reunion. Her militarism combines with ancestor worship and a quasi-chivalric, quasi-medieval backdrop to create Jewett's New England (and, we will see, feminist) version of the late-nineteenth-century vogue for knight-errantry, Anglo-Saxon manhood, and the martial ideal. New arrivals at the reunion are met by Bowden men "with a simple kindness that was the soul of chivalry"; the Bowden "troop" marches in ranks of four, led by "marshal" Santin; they sit at their outdoor feast much as "their ancestors may have sat in the great hall of some old French house in the Middle Ages, when battles and sieges and processions and feasts were familiar things" (pp. 99, 105). The Bowden family might as well be one of the many fraternal organizations — among them the Knights of Columbus and the Ku Klux Klan — that flourished during this period of growing U.S. interest in expansion overseas. The semimythological pasts constructed by such groups, as well as in popular romances and regional literature (such as Jewett's), fulfilled conflicting desires for both escape from and distanced confrontation with anxieties (over "immigrant hordes" at home and a new American empire abroad) of the present.

So, on the one hand, Jewett puts the Bowdens on the road to reunion, sharing dominant cultural vocabularies and values; but on the other, she has the predominantly female clan supplant it with a road of their own, or what amounts to a feminist nationalism. Like the gender confusion and inversion displayed in various ways throughout the Littlepage and Fosdick narratives, the reunion episode brings together spheres that are constructed as culturally separate, in this case the national/public and the female/private. Mothers and ministers are on equal footing in this nationalist vision, accorded places of honor both in the family procession and at table: "It choked me right up," says Mrs. Todd, "to see mother at the head, walkin' with the ministers" (p. 101). If mother as "queen" and "mistress" rules "this great day," reshaping but not rejecting the gender hierarchy, so too does the Bowden militarism partially undercut itself, associated as it is with the pathetic, failed soldier Santin and his ceremonial gestures so disproportionate to their object.

Moreover, the reunion culminates in Chapter 19, "The Feast's End," with a merger of patriotic and culinary display, the ritualistic consumption of American pies that stresses the baking, and its female artistry, as much as the ceremony of eating itself. The pies verge on being self-consuming artifacts, which, when eaten, register discord rather than harmony, abrupt ends rather than ritualistic returns. Mrs. Todd and the narrator consume the words "Bowden Reunion" on an apple pie, leaving only an "undecipherable fragment" (p. 108). But "the most renowned essay in cookery" was a gingerbread model of the old Bowden house, the center of a striking process of ritualistic dismemberment and reincorporation. Not merely "consumed," the house "fell into ruin at the feast's end," and this house divided is then "shared by a great part of the assembly, not without seriousness, and as if it were a pledge and a token of loyalty" (p. 108). Lest we rest on this ceremonial recognition and reconciliation of division, the feast does not stop here, but rather ends with the narrator recounting her deflating meeting with the maker of the gingerbread house. " 'It wasn't all I expected it would be,' she said sadly, as many an artist had said before her of his work" (p. 109).

Just so, the whole reunion episode contains its own critique, both enacting and supplanting the dominant cultural nationalism – but from the female point of view. Jewett's feminism locates a place where she can be critical of the culture within which she speaks. Throughout the central Chapter 18, "The Bowden Reunion," the grand pretensions of this event are simultaneously articulated, "not without seriousness," and exposed. The Mari' Harris/"Chinee" conversation reminds us at the outset of this event that the Bowdens do not always embrace "strange folks" other than their own. Not insignificantly, this discussion is immediately followed by a detailed look at the "particular animosities" within the family. Mrs. Todd confesses that she "always dreads seeing some o' the folks," particularly one of her husband's cousins ("I hate her just the same as I always did"; p. 104). Even the narrator, generally an uncritical Bowden family admirer, experiences a "moment's uneasiness," a cloud that momentarily passes but returns in an extended elegy at the chapter's end to the Bowdens as an unused "reserve force of society." First Santin Bowden and then Mrs. Todd had appeared as "cramped" (by his trade) and "limited" (to her "heavy domesticity") (pp. 101, 105). Finally, however, it is all of them:

> It was not the first time that I was full of wonder at the waste of human ability in this world, as a botanist wonders at the wastefulness of nature. . . . More than one face among the Bowdens showed that only opportunity and stimulus were lacking, – a narrow set of circumstances had caged a fine able character and held it captive. (pp. 106–7)

The endnote of Jewett's feminist nationalism lingers not on patriotic memory but on the costs paid by the "reserve force of society" that, by implication, makes possible its continued existence. Oddly, then, it turns out that, after all, Jewett is participating in the decline-of-New-England trope. But she does so neither entirely in the impoverished, antifemale mode of Berthoff and Parrington nor in the celebratory "women's" mode of the revisionist feminists. Rather, *Country* creates and then debates conflicting images of the past in order to critique new social and sexual relations emerging in the present. Among these new arrangements would be not only the threats posed by domestic immigration and global expansion, but also the possibilities opened up (and closed) by the New Woman. In Jewett's *Country*, as in so much regional literature, the point of constructing a more harmonious, "imaginary" past is to look both away from and toward the disturbing present. Similarly Janus-faced is the category of regionalism itself, which constructs region as both separate from and engaged with nation. In literary history, "regionalism" has had its necessary development as a separate sphere, a "minor" literature with unique characteristics of its own, much as the feminist revisions of Jewett celebrated *Country* as a specifically female sphere of love and ritual. It is time, however, for these worlds apart to be transculturated, as it were, admitted back into the fold of their dialogue with the dominant culture. Only such a fully historicized context enables us to see the nation in Jewett's country.

NOTES

1. T. J. Jackson Lears, *No Place of Grace: Antimodernism and the Transfor-mation of American Culture, 1880–1920* (New York: Pantheon, 1981). A classic of the argument against the female regionalists as a group is Ann Douglas, "The Literature of Impoverishment: The Women Local Colorists in America, 1865–1914," *Women's Studies* 1 (1972): 2–40. For more recent, revisionist views of the concept "minor literature" and the category "regional," see Louis A. Renza, "Introduction: The Question of Minor Literature," in *"A White Heron" and the Question of Minor Literature* (Madison: Univ. of Wisconsin Press, 1984), pp. 3–42, and Eric J. Sundquist, "Realism and Regionalism," in Emory Elliott, ed., *Columbia Literary History of the United States* (New York: Columbia Univ. Press, 1988), pp. 501–3, 509–10. Sundquist, for example, sees critical categories as themselves defined by, not removed from, power: "Those in power (say, white urban males) have more often been judged 'realists,' while those removed from the seats of power (say, Midwesterners, blacks, immigrants, or women) have been categorized as regionalists" (p. 503).

2. Amy Kaplan, "Nation, Region, and Empire," in Emory Elliott, ed., *Columbia History of the American Novel* (New York: Columbia Univ. Press, 1991), p. 242. I am greatly indebted to this essay, which has influenced nearly all aspects of my thinking on Jewett, as will be apparent.

3. Willa Cather, Preface to *The Best Short Stories of Sarah Orne Jewett*, 2 vols. (Boston: Houghton Mifflin, 1925), vol. 1, p. xix.

4. V. L. Parrington, *Main Currents in American Thought*, vol. 3: *The Begin-nings of Critical Realism in America, 1860–1920* (New York: Harcourt, Brace, 1930), and Van Wyck Brooks, *New England: Indian Summer (1865–1915)* (New York: Dutton, 1940). The quotations on Jewett and "women's culture" come respectively from Sandra A. Zagarell, "Narrative of Community: The Identification of a Genre," *Signs* 13 (1988): 498–527; Josephine Donovan, *New England Local Color Liter-ature: A Woman's Tradition* (New York: Ungar, 1983); and Elizabeth Ammons, "Going in Circles: The Female Geography of Jewett's *Coun-try of the Pointed Firs*," *Studies in the Literary Imagination* 16 (1983): 83–92. I would like to note that both Zagarell's and Ammons's argu-ments have changed, as reflected in their essays in this volume.

5. The escape-from-time thesis comes from Josephine Donovan, "Sarah Orne Jewett's Critical Theory: Notes toward a Feminine Literary Mode," in Gwen L. Nagel, ed., *Critical Essays on Sarah Orne Jewett*

(Boston: Hall, 1984), p. 223. The Jewett passage is from *The Country of the Pointed Firs and Other Stories*, ed. Mary Ellen Chase; intro. Marjorie Pryse (New York: Norton, 1982), p. 2. All subsequent page references will be cited in the text.

6. Among the war-related stories are two set in the South, "The Mistress of Sydenham Plantation" (*Atlantic Monthly*, August 1888) and "A War Debt" (*Harper's* magazine, January 1895). Two others concern northern veterans reminiscing about the war, "Decoration Day" (*Harper's* magazine, June 1892) and "Peach-tree Joe" (*Californian Illustrated* magazine, July 1893). On Jewett and race, see Chapter 2 by Sandra Zagarell, this volume. Jewett, "Looking Back on Girlhood," *Youth's Companion* 65 (January 7, 1892), 6.

7. Sundquist, "Realism and Regionalism," p. 508.

8. Paul Buck, *The Road to Reunion, 1865–1900* (Boston: Little, Brown, 1937).

9. Warner Berthoff, "The Art of Jewett's *Country of the Pointed Firs*," *New England Quarterly* 32 (1959); rpt. in *Fiction and Events: Essays in Criticism and Literary History* (New York: Dutton, 1971), p. 254. Ammons, "Going in Circles," pp. 90–1.

10. Kaplan, "Nation, Region, and Empire," p. 242.

11. On her narrative of transvestism, see Chapter 3 by Michael Bell, this volume. Two characteristic examples of other Jewett stories of gender reversal are the comic "An Autumn Holiday" (*Harper's* magazine, October 1880), originally titled "Miss Daniel Gunn," after its transvestite hero/heroine, an old sea captain who believes he is his dead sister Patience; and "Tom's Husband" (*Atlantic Monthly*, February 1882), a story in which husband and wife agree to switch roles, he doing housework, she going out to work, because she is "too independent and self-reliant for a wife; it would seem at first thought that she needed a wife herself more than she did a husband."

12. See Chapter 2 by Zagarell, this volume.

13. W. E. B. Du Bois, "The Conservation of Races," in Philip Foner, ed., *W. E. B. Du Bois Speaks* (New York: Pathfinder Press, 1970). Subsequent page references are cited in the text.

Notes on Contributors

Elizabeth Ammons is Professor of English and of American Studies at Tufts University. She is the author of *Conflicting Stories: American Women Writers at the Turn into the Twentieth Century* (1991) and *Edith Wharton's Argument with America* (1980). She has published many essays on U.S. women writers and is the editor of a number of volumes, including *Short Fiction by Black Women, 1900–1920* (1991), *How Celia Changed Her Mind and Other Stories by Rose Terry Cooke* (1986), and *Critical Essays on Harriet Beecher Stowe* (1980).

Michael Davitt Bell is J. Leland Miller Professor of American History, Literature and Eloquence at Williams College, where he teaches courses in English and American Studies. His published works include *The Development of American Romance: The Sacrifice of Relation* (1980) and *The Problem of American Realism: Studies in the Cultural History of a Literary Idea* (1993), and he has edited a collection of Sarah Orne Jewett's work for the Library of America.

Susan Gillman teaches World Literature and Cultural Studies at the University of California, Santa Cruz. She is the author of *Dark Twins: Imposture and Identity in Mark Twain's America* (1989) and is currently working on a book titled *The American Race Melodramas, 1877–1915*.

June Howard teaches in the Department of English and the Women's Studies and American Culture programs at the University of Michigan, Ann Arbor. She is the author of *Form and History in American Literary Naturalism* (1985) and is at work on a long manuscript with the working title "Making the Family Whole:

119

Gender, Genre and Collaboration in Early Twentieth-Century America."

Sandra A. Zagarell, Professor of English at Oberlin College, is editor of *The Morgesons and Other Writings, Published and Unpublished* by Elizabeth Stoddard (with Lawrence Buell) and *A New Home, Who'll Follow?* by Caroline Kirkland. She has published essays on British and American literature and is at work on an extended study of fictional representations of community in nineteenth-century American literature.

Selected Bibliography

The Country of the Pointed Firs originally appeared as a serial in the *Atlantic Monthly* from January through September 1896; it was published as a book in the same year by Houghton Mifflin. The edition cited in this volume is *The Country of the Pointed Firs and Other Stories,* ed. Mary Ellen Chase, intro. Marjorie Pryse (New York: Norton, 1982).

Ammons, Elizabeth. "Finding Form: Narrative Geography and *The Country of the Pointed Firs.*" Chapter 4 of *Conflicting Stories: American Women Writers at the Turn into the Twentieth Century.* New York: Oxford Univ. Press, 1991, pp. 44–58.

Brodhead, Richard H. "Jewett, Regionalism, and Writing as Women's Work." Chapter 5 of *Cultures of Letters: Scenes of Reading and Writing in Nineteenth-Century America.* Chicago: Univ. of Chicago Press, 1993, pp. 142–76.

Cary, Richard. *Sarah Orne Jewett.* New York: Twayne, 1962.

Cary, Richard, ed. *Appreciation of Sarah Orne Jewett: Twenty-nine Interpretive Essays.* Waterville, Me.: Colby College Press, 1973.

   Sarah Orne Jewett Letters, rev. ed. Waterville, Me.: Colby College Press, 1967.

Cather, Willa. "148 Charles Street." *Not Under Forty.* New York: Knopf, 1936.

Donovan, Josephine. *New England Local Color Literature: A Women's Tradition.* New York: Frederick Ungar, 1983.

   Sarah Orne Jewett. New York: Frederick Ungar, 1980.

Fields, Annie. *The Letters of Sarah Orne Jewett.* Boston: Houghton Mifflin, 1911.

Frost, John Eldridge. *Sarah Orne Jewett.* Kittery Point, Me.: Gundalow Club, 1960.

Hohmann, Marti. "Sarah Orne Jewett to Lily Munger: Twenty-three Letters." *Colby Library Quarterly* 22, no. 1 (March 1986): 28–35.

Matthiessen, F. O. *Sarah Orne Jewett.* Boston: Houghton Mifflin, 1929.

Mobley, Marilyn Sanders. *Folk Roots and Mythic Wings in Sarah Orne Jewett and Toni Morrison: The Cultural Function of Narrative.* Baton Rouge: Louisiana State Univ. Press, 1991.

Nagel, Gwen L., ed. *Critical Essays on Sarah Orne Jewett.* Boston: G. K. Hall, 1984.

Nagel, Gwen Lindberg. *"Sarah Orne Jewett: A Reference Guide* – An Update." *American Literary Realism, 1879–1910* 17, no. 2 (Autumn 1984): 228–63.

Nagel, Gwen L., and James Nagel, comps. *Sarah Orne Jewett: A Reference Guide.* Boston: G. K. Hall, 1978.

O'Brien, Sharon. *Willa Cather: The Emerging Voice.* New York: Oxford Univ. Press, 1987.

Pryse, Marjorie. "Archives of Female Friendship and the 'Way' Jewett Wrote." *New England Quarterly* 66, no. 1 (March 1993): 47–66.

Renza, Louis. *"A White Heron" and the Question of Minor Literature.* Madison: Univ. of Wisconsin Press, 1984.

Roman, Judith. *Annie Adams Fields: The Spirit of Charles Street.* Bloomington: Indiana Univ. Press, 1990.

Roman, Margaret. *Sarah Orne Jewett: Reconstructing Gender.* Tuscaloosa: Univ. of Alabama Press, 1992.

Romines, Ann. *The Home Plot: Women, Writing and Domestic Ritual.* Amherst: Univ. of Massachusetts Press, 1992.

Sherman, Sarah Way. *Sarah Orne Jewett, an American Persephone.* Hanover, N.H.: Univ. Press of New England, 1989.

Spofford, Harriet Prescott. *A Little Book of Friends.* Boston: Little, Brown, 1916.

Weber, Clara Carter, and Carl J. Weber, comps. *A Bibliography of the Published Writings of Sarah Orne Jewett.* Waterville, Me.: Colby College Press, 1949.

Westbrook, Perry D. *Acres of Flint: Sarah Orne Jewett and Her Contemporaries.* Metuchen, N.J.: Scarecrow Press, 1951; rev. ed., 1981.